The Americans in Australia

The AMERICANS in Australia

Ray Aitchison

Australian Ethnic Heritage Series
General Editor: Michael Cigler

AE Press
Melbourne 1986

Australasian Educa Press Pty Ltd
(Incorporated in Victoria)
74 Railway Road, Blackburn, 3130
Tel. (03) 878 0466

First published 1986

THE AMERICANS IN AUSTRALIA
is a volume in the
Australian Ethnic Heritage Series
General Editor: Michael Cigler, Melbourne.

National Library of Australia
Cataloguing-in-publication entry
Aitchison, Ray.
   The Americans in Australia.

   Bibliography.
   Includes index.
   ISBN 0 86787 208 X

   1. Americans — Australia. I. Title.
   (Series: Australian ethnic heritage series).

994'.00413

Typeset by Leader Composition, Blackburn, Victoria
Printed in Australia by Brown Prior Anderson, Burwood, Victoria

Foreword

Most Australians and Americans I know are aware of the longstanding links between their countries. A sense of strained siblinghood, somewhat like that between twins raised in different homes, has marked their shared history. These feelings, ranging from love to hate, sometimes have been reflected in mutual attitudes and preconceptions. Once modified by direct contact with real people, these ill-formed sentiments usually change. The words and stories of numerous Americans – the Yankees who came and stayed – reveal the process in this book.

Less well known, and much less frequently discussed, is the parallel movement of people between the two countries. This migration stream commenced with the arrival of Cook in this, then entirely Aboriginal, continent. People born in the United States and their children have been an important minority in Australia, both in terms of numbers and their contribution, throughout the last two centuries. The following chapters provide an engaging view of this continuing role.

Between the end of the Second World War and December 1983, it has been estimated that 70 900 immigrants from the USA came to Australia, nearly 2 percent of the more than 4 million people who arrived in that period. To put that in context, these 'Americans' equalled roughly half the number who came from Germany (141 000) and from New Zealand (136 700). In those years the number of Americans who arrived in Australia exceeded those from Vietnam, Lebanon, India, South Africa, or Malaysia. Despite the numbers, 'we' have been a fairly invisible minority to most people, including 'ourselves'. There are some, perhaps obvious, reasons for this and others, more subtle, which are suggested in the following pages.

Two half-truths about the 'ease of accommodation' among Americans in Australia warrant mention. One is that the cultures of these nations are fundamentally similar. They are, of course, but they are quite dissimilar in many ways as well. Many of these differences are much more real than apparent. The second half-truth is that the analogies of the two derive drom a shared Anglo-Saxon heritage and common language. This is also, of course, true. However, it is only the beginning of a complex story. Another, less emphasised, common denominator is the shared tradition of a heritage based on numerous cultures other than the obvious one.

It is barely a decade since America's Bicentennial and on the brink of Australia's. Both will have been important celebrations and marked by some friction provoked by internal diversity. In both cases this friction has a chance to generate as much light as it has heat. Both countries are increasingly mature members in the family of nations. For most American-Australians the tensions of a young siblinghood have ripened into a deep and respectful affection.

As an American in Australia, this book is of great interest to me. As a student of multiculturalism, by training, habit and choice, I see Aitchison's work as both useful and informative.

Regardless of the circumstances or accident which has brought your attention to this page, I encourage you to read on.

Anthony C. Colson, Ph.D
Principal Research Fellow
Australian Institute of Multicultural Affairs

Contents

Sources and Acknowledgments

The author would like to express his thanks to the many people who have assisted in the collection of material for this book, in particular those who contributed to its liveliness via interviews.

Further, the author gratefully acknowledges the permission of the following copyright holders to reproduce material and pictures used in this book:
Archives of South Australia, Department of Immigration and Ethnic Affairs, John Oxley Library, Mitchell Library, John Fairfax and Sons Pty Ltd, Joe Bradshaw, and Paul Naco.

Introduction

Americans have been closely involved in the affairs of Australia for almost two centuries. The first American traders to visit Australia arrived in 1791, only three years after Governor Phillip founded Sydney. Soon others were helping convicts to escape from the Sydney penal settlement, and Yankees were engaging in the notorious rum trade that corrupted the small community.

Piratical seal-hunters and whalers from the United States cruised Australian waters and fought local crews for the best hunting areas.

Americans were among the pioneers of Australian agriculture, mining and secondary industries, and were active in commerce. Miners from California joined in the great Australian gold rush of the mid-nineteenth century. Other Americans began the Cobb and Co. stage coach business along the lines of Wells Fargo of the American Wild West. They built railways, telegraph lines, and they improved shipping facilities. They became involved in early Australian politics and distinguished themselves in architecture and the arts.

During the Second World War, one million US servicemen trained or took their leave in Australia. After the war, American businessmen helped develop modern financial institutions in Australia, or invested money in national engineering projects, mining, ranching or retailing. New settlers from the United States contributed to scientific advancement. American teachers got jobs in Australian schools. Entertainers from New York or Los Angeles made new show business names for themselves with audiences in Sydney or Melbourne.

In this book, the opinions and experiences of Americans in modern Australia are presented along with the stories of Americans of the past. Their frank observations cover many topics. Obviously they could only measure their lives in Australia against what they had known and left behind in the United States. They had interesting things to say about the United States too.

Americans in Australia often have been passionate advocates for republicanism. In earlier times their presence in Australia worried British administrators. Modern American settlers interviewed for this book were more cautious about it, but most of them still thought that Australia should become a republic as quickly as possible. Some objected to having to swear allegiance to a monarch in Britain at Australian citizenship ceremonies. Others were of the opinion that the granting of British imperial titles to Australians created pretensions of rank for some above the rest of the community and had social and business advantages for the recipients and that this weakened Australia's claims that it was an egalitarian country.

A former Prime Minister of Australia, Sir John Gorton, disclosed that his American wife once went to the Minister for Immigration at that time, Arthur Calwell, and asked him how she could become an Australian citizen. 'Calwell told her she could not do it unless she gave up her American citizenship, so my wife told him in no uncertain terms what he should do. She remained a US citizen until the day she died.'

One could not imagine the ladylike Bettina Gorton having been rude in her conversation with Arthur Calwell, but that was the way her husband described the incident years afterwards. It is relevant to mention here that Calwell was the grandson of an American goldminer who settled in Australia after the gold rush.

Disillusioned Americans left the United States in the 1970s and 1980s to escape aspects of American life they disliked – for example, pollution of the environment by industries, crime in the cities, or 'the rat race' in their jobs. Others were angry about

government policies or actions in the United States and emigrated as a form of protest. Many to whom we spoke remained
critics of America, yet none thought that this was disloyalty to
their native country. Maureen Maloy from Portland, Oregon,
who had been in Australia fifteen years, told us, 'In the US
school system you are taught to speak up and look at things
critically and discuss them critically and I guess that is what I do.'

When the suggestion was put to American settlers, however,
that they should renounce their US citizenship after long
residence and become naturalised Australian citizens, it seemed
to strike some as an invitation to commit treason, no matter
what other reasons they offered for not wishing to do it. Of all
immigrant groups in Australia, Americans have been probably
the most reluctant to transfer their citizenship legally from their
former country to their new one. Often they admitted to us that
if anything went wrong for them in Australia they wanted to
have an easy re-entry into the United States. Americans have
died in Australia of old age, leaving their US passports amongst
their last possessions and their most treasured – a bridge home
to their native land had it been needed, but also illustrative of
their pride in having been Americans.

Although some arriving in Australia have had angry personal
reasons for leaving the United States, by far the most common
has been the arrival of people seeking to broaden their experience in a 'frontier' country but not intending to stay permanently.

Survey
The results of a sample survey of Americans living in Australia
were published in 1976 by Jan De Amicis of the Department of
Sociology, University of Massachusetts. De Amicis came to the
conclusion that Americans usually did not make decisions to
migrate to Australia. Their permanent residence in Australia
happened almost accidentally.

According to De Amicis, most Americans in Australia arrived
with the intention of returning home eventually. Often they

remained unaware of the subtle changes occurring in their lives resulting from experiences of marriage, family and work.

De Amicis said:

> The fundamental similarities between Australian and American life make their adjustment problems in Australia few and mild. They often lose their paramount sense of being foreigners. As everyday life becomes increasingly normalised, they encounter normal contingencies which often encourage or demand the extension of increasingly significant ties and commitments. Ties to America weaken and are replaced by corresponding ties to Australia.
>
> More often than not, Americans arriving in Australia have not severed their personal and career links with the United States. Rather, they have suspended them almost in the same fashion as Americans moving temporarily from one part of the United States to another. The almost insidious ease with which Americans blend into everyday life in Australia can undermine intentions to return home for every week and month they remain.

In a paper, delivered at a symposium on ethnicity and migration held by the Australian and New Zealand Journal of Sociology, Jan De Amicis observed that Americans suffered from fewer and lighter adjustment problems than any other major group of immigrants in Australia. They did not confront Australia as a totally foreign, completely different, culture. De Amicis said:

> Quite the reverse. Most Americans remark how similar to the United States Australia seems to be. Australia is basically identical to the States in most respects. Institutions, brand names, modes of dress, patterns of interpersonal communication and so on. Everyday life in Australia seems to differ from that of America in degree rather than in kind. Adjustment problems are mild and occur in

separate spheres of the immigrant's life. Thus the American immigrant does not have to learn everything all over again. As an obvious example, he not only speaks English, but understands and is understood by Australians in terms of easy familiarity.

De Amicis said that a nearly exhaustive listing of adjustment problems for Americans included: Lower wage scales, shortage and/or expense of consumer goods, loneliness, driving automobiles on the left, problems associated with shopping (different names for familiar items, different store hours), the absence of business contacts, the accent, the slower pace and laxity of work and business procedures, the absence of central heating in houses, the quality of service in public areas such as restaurants, some patterns of conversation, food, the general cost of living, and male (chauvinist) attitudes towards women.

Respondents to De Amicis' survey rarely mentioned more than one or two of these items of readjustment, and few mentioned exactly the same problems. De Amicis concluded that these difficulties were not objectively troublesome features of Australia which faced all Americans, but were selectively perceived and encountered. Many Americans in Australia had difficulty recalling any adjustment problems at all, so superficial did they seem at the time encountered and in retrospect, at the time of the survey interview.

Americans finding work in Australia in university lecturing, secondary school teaching, advertising, art, sales, hotels and travel, often became career-oriented in Australia as a result of their rapid progression through the ranks of their professions. De Amicis found that rapid career progression was typically quite unexpected among the Americans surveyed and forced many of them to postpone their planned return to the States indefinitely.

Interviews
We interviewed Tom Dixon from Ames, Iowa. He had become a

senior conservator at the National Gallery of Art in Melbourne. Dixon said:

> Australia is not easily compared with the United States although some people unwisely attempt to do it. The United States consists of half a dozen very different regions. Americans travelling across the United States are likely to experience dissimilarities just as striking to them as they would find if they went all the way across the Pacific to Australia. For example, I am sure that New Yorkers would feel less at home in Colorado than would Australians, because the Colorado region and its people seem to me to have more in common with Australians somehow.

Dixon said he had found that Australians often had stereotyped notions about Americans, gained from American television and movies: 'A lot of that entertainment is the garbage of American culture. No wonder Australians get bad ideas about us.'

He said he had gone to Australia because his career in the United States had been at a crossroads.

> A reverse discrimination was working in my profession. A female or a coloured person was more likely to be promoted than a white male. I'm opposed to discrimination, including that particular type. In fact, I'm a representative now at government discussions in Australia on equal opportunities for employment on a non-discriminatory level.

Sarah Rankin, 26, from Boston, worked for the Computer Corporation of America and was sent to Australia by her company in 1982 to help the corporation compete for a government contract. She was successful, but after two further short visits to Australia she resigned her job. She crossed the

Pacific again to work for an Australian company at less money. She explained to us why she had done it:

> The puritan work ethic in Boston probably is stronger than in most other places in America. I had to work until eight or nine every night in my job in Boston and had no time for anything else. I knew that in Australia they consider you've done a good day's work if you go to five or six o'clock in the evenings. There is time left over for other things apart from work. I wanted a better balanced life.

Jay Pendarvis moved from Immokallee in Florida where he was a rancher. Land in Florida had become too valuable for cattle-raising or for farming so he sold out and investigated less developed countries, including areas of South America. In 1967, he visited friends in the Australian Northern Territory and thought that it resembled the American Wild West of the last century – all those wide-open, unfenced grasslands. He liked it and stayed to raise cattle and to capture and market wild buffaloes. 'I'm still an American citizen,' he said in 1985, 'but I've been so busy in Australia that I've never been back to the United States, even for a holiday.'

Pendarvis was divorced from his first wife, Irma, an American woman, in 1979. 'After our divorce, Irma returned to the United States but after a while she was back again in the Northern Territory. You could say that the Northern Territory has real fascination for Americans like us.'

Pendarvis became a national figure in Australia in 1985 when union officials set up a picket line to shut down his abattoir. The union claimed that his work contract with his employees was breaking union award conditions. Pendarvis said, 'My men can't understand the union's attitude. Some are making a thousand dollars a week.'

His employees were expelled from union membership, but in August 1985 the meat workers' union had to pay a fine of

$44 000 for contempt of court after losing a long legal battle against Pendarvis. The union also had to pay Pendarvis' legal costs. Australia's unions held nationwide industrial stoppages in protest, including strikes by workers in shipping ports and airlines. Pendarvis struck back by suing the meatworkers union for compensation for lost production and sales during the months his meatworks was besieged by the picket line.

On 1 January 1986, the *Australian* newspaper announced its readers' nomination of Jay Pendarvis as 'Australian of the Year'. The newspaper wrote: 'Pendarvis proved himself a man of courage prepared to risk his livelihood and his future for a principle in which be believed.'

Pendarvis said he had settled in Australia because he thought it had the most potential of any country in the English-speaking world but he went on,

> I cannot understand why this great country, rich in natural resources is content to sell its resources to foreign nations and then buy them back in the form of finished products that we could produce ourselves. Where is our national pride?

According to Dr Jon Ables from Oklahoma, a two-tiered education system in Australia has helped develop class division in the community.

> The first impression an American gets is that Australia is more egalitarian than the United States, but there is a subtle difference. The class division in Australia is social. In America it is mostly financial.

Dr Ables, 47, the director of the National Radio Astronomy Observatory at Parkes in New South Wales, also had been in Australia since 1967. His three children had been educated in Australian schools and universities. His own father and mother were teachers in the United States. He said:

The two-tiered system in Australia begins at primary school level when children are sent to public schools or private schools. Heavily financed private schools are for the elite – and it is a hereditary elite because parents who went to private schools send their children there. The Australian public sees its public school system to be inferior to the private school system.

As an American I strongly disagree with this situation. It perpetuates a class division in Australia – often covert or ignored – but real. It is an 'old boy' system and works behind the scenes.

American teachers working in Australian schools told us they considered there was scant regard to teaching children Australian history, government, or much about the Australian Constitution. Nor was there enough accent on patriotism. Their criticisms about studies of government processes – or lack of it – certainly deserved attention. In the Australian federal elections of December 1984 a large percentage of voters failed to mark their ballot papers properly. Later a Roy Morgan survey asked the public to name both Houses of the Australian Federal Parliament. Thirty-six percent could not name the House of Representatives and 40 percent could not name the Senate. Of those surveyed, another 24 percent could not name either House of Parliament!

An American who became a naturalised Australian was history professor Dan Potts, of Monash University in Melbourne. In 1976, he warned Australians against allowing their political leaders to become too powerful. Other Americans have commented since that, in their opinions, Australians did not have enough local controls over their elected representatives, except at elections, because political party machines selected candidates to represent them, got them elected and managed them.

Norm Sanders from California, who was elected to the Australian Senate, had another point of view. He said that candidates in election campaigns in the United States had to sell their souls to sponsors and that 'even a dog-catcher has to buy his way into office'. Sanders, who is quoted more fully later in this book, said he was surprised when he discovered that in Australia an ordinary citizen without much money could be elected to Parliament.

But then we met Ronald Gaudreau from New York, and he said that too many Australians seemed to accept that their governments knew what was best for them.

> Americans don't fall for that. They don't trust governments to run their lives and they like less government. The dynamism of the United States comes upwards from the involvement of the people; but since coming to Australia I have often thought that people here expect direction and help to come down to them from government, and wait for it to happen.

A church group in San Francisco sent Pastor Jim Dykes to Sydney to establish a community support system to help AIDS victims.

Dykes told us:

> We knew that the AIDS epidemic was going to take the same course in Australia as it had in America, and with the same degree of human suffering. From our experience earlier with the problems associated with AIDS it was thought that I could be useful in Australia.

Pastor Dykes set up a community support system in Sydney called Ankali, an Aboriginal word meaning friend. Ankali provided intensive counselling for AIDS victims. Dykes said:

> They are devastated people on two levels. They are facing death but also feel that they have a terrible stigma. They can find themselves being regarded with the same

Reverend Jim Dykes.

horror that the public reserved for lepers in the Middle Ages.

Our counsellors have tried to modify terror into practical action and acceptance of preventative education. The Australian concept of mateship has been useful in this field. Mateship means going to the rescue of a friend in time of crisis. We have found that community support for AIDS victims in Australia has been practical whereas in the United States often it has been emotional.

In 1985, the Australian Minister for Health, Dr Blewett, praised Pastor Dykes and others in the Ankali counselling service for their work in the AIDS epidemic. Jim Dykes said that his work in Australia had been 'low key' because he was an American and there were differences between Australians and the people of his own country. He said:

Australians tend to express anger indirectly, often making it difficult for others to know why they are angry. It's almost as if they guide their anger in indirect ways to disguise the real reason for it. If I were given a guess I would say that this is because of an historic fear in Australia of authoritarian figures who must not be confronted directly. Australians tend to take out their anger on something else or somebody else. If they are angry about having become ill, for example, they often will direct their anger against hospital administration or personnel, or even against visitors to their bedside, instead of admitting to themselves that they are mad about being ill.

Robert Morrison, an organic chemist, was invited to Australia in 1978 from Boston to establish a study course at the Canberra College of Advanced Education. He said:

It was a cultural shock for myself and my wife. There

are significant differences between the cultures of the people in Australia and their attitudes towards various things, and what we had known back home, but a lot of the differences we liked. My wife and I have found that Australians are more honest than Americans. They are not as intense. Tensions in the United States overwhelm so many Americans. Australia is not as violent a country as America either. That alone is a good enough reason for us to stay here.

American basketball players have become new sporting heroes in Australia. By 1986 about 500 Americans were competing in top-level Australian basketball teams. Many more were playing in lower-grade competitions. American stars in the sport included Herb McEachin who had a permanent resident permit, an Australian wife and two young children, and no plans to return to the United States.

McEachin had played basketball for his adopted country against teams from 20 other nations and had toured with Australians in Malaysia, Singapore and Canada. He said he had many Australian friends but occasionally encountered racial prejudice because he was a black man.

The difference between racial prejudice in Australia and at home is that it is less open in Australia. If a racist doesn't like you in America because you're black, most likely he'll let you know. In Australia they smile and conceal what they're thinking.

McEachin was coaching a junior girl player in Canberra whose mother was always there, watching and supportive. One day the girl told McEachin that her mother thought he was a terrific coach but she would never want him to visit her home.

McEachin: 'I prefer the attitude of the Ku Klux Klan. Their open hostility is more honest.'

Al Green, 28, another black American basketballer, was one

of a family of ten children and grew up in the ghetto of the
Bronx, New York. He became a naturalised Aussie in 1984 and
settled in Adelaide. Did he miss the excitement of New York?

> Sometimes I do – at weekends. The rest of the week they
> can keep it in New York. Adelaide is home to me now. It's
> laid back and I like it. You can leave your door open and
> you won't get robbed . . . Not as much, anyhow . . .

In view of the reluctance of other Americans to do it why had
he become a naturalised Australian?

> When you leave a place they forget you and it's no good
> going back to start again. I'm setting myself up for the
> future here . . . When I gave up my American citizenship
> it didn't hit me until after. My mother wrote and said she
> wanted for me what I want and that made me feel better.
> Mom prays for me.

Sheri Pigott, also black and from New York, did miss the
excitement of the Big Apple.

> I grew up in Manhattan on the lower east side and there
> were Greeks and Italians, Puerto Ricans, Blacks and Jews.
> It was electric. I was getting all this culture from all these
> different people: music, food, religions, social customs –
> it was just there. In Australia I find a lot of separation
> between different ethnic groups.

A former Chicago businessman, William Thorne, said in
Brisbane:

> America probably is a more multi-ethnic country than
> Australia but its strong emphasis on US citizenship and its
> rights is the cement holding the population together.
> The US still has its racial problems, God knows, but I am

Herb McEachin, No. 15 (Courtesy P Naco).

of the opinion that Australia is creating its own brand of racial trouble for the future by going too soft on the values of Australian citizenship and not welding separate ethnic groups more closely together. A multi-national country is a lot more divided than a multi-ethnic one and can expect a heap of racial trouble, sooner or later.

Asked to explain more clearly what he meant, Thorne added:

All Americans, regardless of their ethnic origins, skin colour, land of birth, or religious beliefs are entitled to expect and receive equal justice and equal opportunities and all the other rights and freedoms attainable through US citizenship. No less and no more than that. In return, we have our responsibilities to our country as citizens. Citizenship is not sufficiently understood and appreciated in Australia. It is too casual here. Too many foreigners are allowed to stay too long without taking out their citizenship papers. Kids are not being taught enough about it at school.

Bob Turner from Santa Barbara, coached basketball teams in New South Wales. He tried to persuade audiences to sing the national anthem 'Advance Australia Fair' before his matches began. They rose to their feet self-consciously but often remained standing in silence while Turner played the anthem over the public address system. Turner came to the conclusion that few Australians knew the words – so he had the verses of Advance Australia Fair printed on his basketball programmes and hired vocalists to help it along. It worked marginally. He suspected many people were humming it though. He said:

Australians are quieter and more reserved than Americans as a general rule. They don't have to live and work under such intense pressures. Americans newly arriving have to learn this and modify their more aggressive style and tone it down.

He believed that because the United States had many more millions of people and greater competition they were raised from infancy to understand that life was going to be combative. As a result most of those arriving in Australia brought with them an inbuilt commitment to succeed in whatever they undertook. Often that gave them a winning edge against more relaxed Australians.

Quite a few of the Americans we interviewed were convinced that there was some kind of national inferiority complex in Australia. 'Little careless comments by any visitor to Australia can trigger it off. They are a prickly lot and we have to learn to guard our tongues,' Herb McEachin said.

Maureen Maloy, who tried unsuccessfully to run for local government in Tasmania, said: 'As soon as I opened my mouth I offended people. It was my American accent. People seemed to think I was Big Brother telling them what to do.'

Senator Norm Sanders also mentioned the handicap of his American accent in his life in Australia, and the radio astronomer, Dr Jon Ables, was among those American settlers who had come to the conclusion that Australia was a country suffering from a national inferiority complex. 'I think it is a great pity,' he said.

In 1976, we were in Washington and witnessed the pride of American citizens in the two hundredth birthday of their republic. The American Bicentennial celebrations were exuberant and flamboyant but wholehearted. We heard Americans making fun of the celebrations but there was no mistaking the positive national spirit in which they were being held. Australians are entitled to feel similar pride of nationhood and we believe they do feel it although perhaps they are less demonstrative than Americans. They are often ready to put themselves down but won't allow foreigners to do it. Beneath their laconic and deceptively casual manner they are proud to be Aussies. And indeed why shouldn't they be? Their country's record over the past two centuries has been one of achievement, overcoming hardships and the numerous disadvantages of geographical isolation.

The former head of the New York City Bicentennial Corporation, Ronald L Gaudreau, adopted Australia as his home in 1982. He had some comments about the coming commemorations in Australia:

> The occasion provides us with opportunities to re-examine national ideals, goals and values. We can attain an increased understanding of the contributions made by all settlers of this country. We can gain an increased awareness of the richness of Australia's cultural heritage and a greater sense of its role and position in the world.

Mr Gaudreau added:

> Immigrants bring with them the cultures of other nations but environment in a new country soon begins to change them into unique forms. That is why Australia is so interesting for people like myself arriving here. Australia is different and has enriched the cultural contributions made by immigrants by adding something uniquely Australian to them.

This book is about those Americans who have contributed to Australia's development during her short history.

1 Sailors, Whalers, Sealers, Rebels

Cook's Men

Did you know that the first three Americans to arrive in Australia made the trip with Captain James Cook? Two of them were willing. The other wanted to be somewhere else.

John Thurmond, a seaman in the sloop, *Outward Bound*, from New York, had arrived in Funchal, the chief port of Madeira. He had gone eagerly ashore to enjoy a sailor's pleasures around the waterfront bars. Unluckily for him, a British vessel, *Endeavour*, happened to be in port. Its captain, James Cook, needed additional crew and sent a press-gang ashore with instructions to shanghai any able-bodied men they could capture.

Compulsory recruitment by press-gang was one of the shore risks a sailor expected in the mid-eighteenth century but Thurmond's dismay when he found himself aboard the Endeavour must have been profound. Relationships between colonial Americans and the British no longer were cordial. An honest New York merchant seaman like Thurmond resented bitterly being commandeered into the Royal British Navy with his wrists tied and a lump on his head.

The other two Americans with Captain Cook were Midshipman Mario Matra, also from New York, and Second Lieutenant John Fore from Virginia. Both were career officers in the British Navy. Few people seriously believed that a revolutionary war would occur in America. Only foolish people would have predicted in 1768 that Great Britain would lose if such an unlikely war did occur.

James Thurmond never saw New York again. With his two compatriots he shared Cook's voyage of discovery to the Pacific and set foot on Australian soil; Thurmond died during the return voyage to England. He was buried at sea.

Eight years after sailing with Cook, Matra wrote to the British Government proposing a scheme for the resettlement in Australia of American refugees. One hundred thousand loyalists had been displaced by the War of Independence. Britain had to find new homes for them.

Matra suggested that American artificers, potters and gardeners should be sent initially to Australia. Women could be obtained from New Caledonia or Tahiti to become their wives. Their livestock could be obtained from the Cape of Good Hope or the Moluccas. Matra suggested that two companies of British marines be sent to protect them.

He wrote that British loyalists born in America, but now without a country, already were conditioned to colonial life and would succeed admirably in an Australian frontierland. The settlement they founded could become a peaceful centre for trade with Eastern Asia, or a wartime base for hostilities against the Dutch colonies of Malaysia, or the Spanish colonies of South America.

Matra raised no objections to convicts being sent to Australia as colonists with the American loyalists, if they were given land to cultivate and never reproached for their former crimes. When British convicts were being sent to America (1750–75) they were sold for a servitude of seven years. When they were being sent to Africa they were also condemned to public labour. Matra reminded the Government that 334 of the 746 British convicts sent to Africa in 1775–76 died, and 271 deserted to no one knew where. Of the remainder no account could be given. Obviously it would serve Britain better to have her convicts working constructively and happily to develop a valuable new Crown colony in Australia than have them slaves as had happened in America and Africa.

Matra's main purpose though was to assist displaced Americans. He wrote:

> This country [Australia] may afford an asylum to those unfortunate American loyalists to whom Great Britain is bound by every tie of honour and gratitude to protect and support, where they may repair their broken fortunes, and again enjoy their former felicity.

In Nova Scotia, James de Lancey, who had been the most important landlord in southern New York State before the war, began enlisting loyalist refugees to resettle in Australia. Admiral Sir George Young of the British Navy submitted a proposal to the Government for a settlement in Australia, similar to the one suggested by Matra. Sir Joseph Banks, who had sailed with Cook, also was interested.

Probably their work was the basis of a paper prepared for Lord Sydney by the Colonial Office, and handed to the British Government in August 1786. This document borrowed many of the ideas and phrases of the written reports submitted earlier by Matra and Sir George Young, but deleted all reference to American loyalists and free settlers. It carried the lengthy and decisive title: 'Heads of a Plan for Effectively Disposing of Convicts, by the Establishment of a Colony in New South Wales'.

American loyalist refugees were not part of the plan.

In 1777, Mario Matra revisited New York to recover whatever was left of his family's property. Afterwards he was employed in the British Diplomatic Service. He became Consul General at Tangier in Morocco in 1786 and died there 20 years later. In Sydney, the suburb of Matraville is named after him.

Lieutenant John Gore was again with Captain Cook on his third and final voyage (1776–79). Once more two other Americans were involved. They were Simeon Woodruff, a gunner's mate, and John Ledyard, a corporal of marines from Connecticut. After Cook's death in the Hawaiian islands, command of the expedition passed to the Virginian, Lieutenant John Gore.

Traders

The War of Independence stopped the monopolistic East India Company from shipping tea and other products from China to the American market. To refill their country's empty teapots, American trading vessels began making epic voyages from their home ports on the Atlantic coast and around the world to China. It became inevitable that the American ships, sooner or later, would begin calling at Britain's new settlement at Sydney on the Australian seaboard.

The first was the *Philadelphia* which arrived on 1 November 1792. Her skipper, Captain Thomas Patrickson had come looking for trade.

A new light burned in the eyes of the convicts. They had been without hope – outcasts in a settlement so remote from the rest of the world that only the British Navy which had put them there could find them again. Now here was an American visitor. A window to the outside world had opened.

The *Philadelphia* had brought to Sydney a cargo of pitch and tar, rum and gin, and some tobacco and beef. Captain Patrickson offered a hard sell. If the British in Sydney would not buy his cargo he would take it elsewhere. What could be fairer than that?

The British East India Company had a monopoly on trade with Asia under British law and Australia was not exempt. On the other hand, Governor Phillip's first duty to his government was to ensure that its colony continued to survive. If he turned away the *Philadelphia* and its cargo, weeks or months would pass before the next British supply ship reached Sydney. The colony needed to encourage independent trading vessels to call, foreign or not, to help overcome the uncertainty of its survival. Phillip bought the *Philadelphia's* cargo and American ships began making Sydney a regular port of call.

The next trading vessel to reach Sydney after the *Philadelphia* was the *Hope* from Rhode Island under the command of Captain Benjamin Page, bringing 7 600 gallons of American rum made from West Indian molasses. At that time, West Indian molasses was supplying 63 distilleries in Massachusetts. With such intense competition, rum-makers were searching the world for new markets for their product. They found one in thirsty Australia.

Governor Phillip had ordered that trade in liquor in the colony should be restricted to those whom he vaguely described as 'proper persons', but Phillip had returned to England before the *Hope* reached Sydney. In temporary command of the colony was an opportunist, Major Francis Grose, Officer-in-Charge of the New South Wales Corps, the garrison regiment and watchdogs over the convicts. Major Grose and his officers pooled their money to buy the *Hope's* cargo of rum. They were confident that they were the proper persons Governor Phillip had mentioned.

Imported rum, much of it from America, became the currency of graft, corruption and degradation in the Australian colony. Convicts sold their food rations for rum; new settlers took rum instead of money for their farm produce. The 'firewater' given to the native aborigines warmed their bellies, befuddled their minds and hastened their ruin.

For the first 20 years of the Sydney settlement its trade was almost exclusively with the United States. Britain's East India Company was not interested in the Australia trade but its monopoly east of Suez kept other British traders away. Not until 1807 did Australia begin a mercantile trade with its Mother Country.

Sixteen American ships had called at Sydney up to 1800, sailing the new triangular Pacific route – to Sydney with rum and other supplies, to Alaska or to the Aleutians for furs, to China for tea and then home to the American Atlantic coast. These commercial voyages by the Americans were sagas of the sea. So valuable were they to the early Australian economy that colonial authorities gave United States vessels of all kinds equal rights with British ships in Australian ports, a most unusual concession. (Later, American ships were restricted to Neutral Bay in Sydney Harbour on a bond of £200 (afterwards £500) to prevent illegal trading and the escape of convicts).

The outbreak of war between Britain and the United States of 1812 put a stop to this fraternisation in the Southern Hemisphere. After the war *Traveller*, an American ship from Canton en route to Timor in 1816, arrived in Sydney, its captain eager to show there were no hard feelings, and ready to resume business.

The Governor of the Australian colony was Major General Lachlan Macquarie. His apparent autocratic ways as the paramount instrument of the British Government had antagonised prominent citizens including the Reverend Benjamin Vale and Mr W.H. Moore, a government solicitor. General Macquarie was temporarily absent on a trip up-country when the *Traveller* anchored, and the Reverend Vale and Mr Moore saw their chance. They arrested the ship as a lawful prize under the British Navigation Act. This was the legislation which had contributed to revolution in America by attempting to restrict all trade between Britain and her colonies to British shipping.

Vale and Moore had calculated their action would anger and compromise the Governor. They were not disappointed. When Macquarie learned what had occurred in his absence he ordered the liberation of the *Traveller* and declared that trade with American vessels must not be hindered in future. He court-martialled the Reverend Vale (Chaplain of the 16th Regiment) for insolent and highly insubordinate behaviour and dismissed the lawyer, Mr Moore, from his government post. Macquarie described the arrest of the *Traveller* as an example of 'factious and illiberal principles'.

The British Government took a legalistic view. It informed Macquarie that the Navigation Act must be strictly applied in Australian ports under British law. All foreign vessels were forbidden to trade with Sydney 'except in cases in which the necessities of the colony may require the relaxation of this general rule'.

Macquarie protested that every colonial governor in Sydney since Captain Phillip had welcomed American vessels as being essential to the comfort and security of the colony. By then about

50 ships from the United States had traded in Sydney in contravention of the Navigation Act and the East India Company monopoly, starting with the *Philadelphia* in 1792.

The British Government stuck by its decision. Regular trade between the United States and the Sydney colony ceased in 1816 and did not resume until the Navigation Laws were relaxed in the 1820s. Indirect trade continued through the transhipment of American goods into British vessels.

Between 1836 and 1843 the first American firm, Kenworthy and Company, became established in Australia and for some years had almost a monopoly on trade with the United States.

The first Australian wool shipped directly to the United States was carried in the *Black Warrior* in 1834. The *Tartar of Boston* took the first shipment of ice to Australia in 1839. It loaded 400 tons but 150 tons melted during the voyage through the tropics.

Whalers and Sealers

About two-thirds of the Australian continent and New Zealand was still unclaimed by the British when the first American whalers and sealers began finding their way into empty bays and inlets in both countries. They set up temporary shore stations. The first time many Australian Aborigines heard the English language being spoken, it had an American accent.

The whale and seal herds of the southern ocean had never been hunted. They were in natural abundance as they had been for thousands of years. In the migration season, whales so packed the Derwent River of Tasmania that the British Governor complained from his home near the river bank that their splashing and spouting left him sleepless at night.

Then came the Americans. In November 1802, Governor King in Sydney wrote to his superiors in London for guidance concerning American whalers and sealers who were infesting Australian waters. Two years later King reported to London that Americans were off the Australian coast in even greater numbers – 'procuring its produce to the evident disadvantage of the colonists'. King complained that the livelihood of 123 Sydney men, exclusive of shipbuilders, artificers and labourers, was being threatened by American competition.

Most of the whaling vessels from the United States were commanded by Nantucket men, far-ranging mariners, eager to fill the holds of their ships with oil and whalebone in the shortest possible time. The American sealers who closely followed them to Australia were just as hard and equally hungry for profits. When they began using Sydney Harbour as a base, discipline in the penal settlement was endangered. Brawls occurred often between the Americans and locals, particularly in the Rocks District of the harbourside. When the Americans were ashore, rowdy men and women crowded Sydney's new rum taverns and thronged the town's narrow streets. Some Sydney convict women rejoiced that the profession in which they had been so well practised in Britain had become profitable again.

In August 1804, Governor King closed Sydney Harbour to American whalers and sealers. He decreed that no aliens would be allowed to reside in the Australian colony without the permission of the Governor or his deputy. King also decided that the employment of British seamen by foreigners would be prohibited. He provided penalties for breaches of these regulations, hoping to maintain law and order, but also to foster local investment and jobs. Industry protectionism thus began quite early in Australia.

Although banned from Sydney, the Americans had the rest of the Australian coastlines to find rough provisions, shelter and water. Some even built new ships from local timber.

The great days of American whaling in the Pacific extended into the 1850s. The Americans hunted sperm whales from boats lowered from ocean-going vessels. They also pursued black whales which had their breeding grounds in the shallow bays of the Tasmanian and New Zealand coasts. These they killed from smaller craft put out from shore or from a vessel at anchor in the bay. The dead whales were towed to a mother ship, or ashore, to be dismembered and boiled down for their oil.

Whalers of many nationalities continued to congregate along the coast of New Zealand until the middle of the nineteenth century. Ships from Salem, Bristol, Le Havre, and Sydney, worked together for months in isolated bays, making their catches and assisting one another. Independence, lawlessness and profit often went together, but so too did co-operation.

In view of Governor King's opposition to the Americans it was ironic that he was forced to use their ships for official business. The penal settlement of Sydney was so isolated from the rest of the world that visiting American vessels were needed, especially when the Napoleonic Wars began disrupting British communications. Additional to their cargoes, American whaling and trading vessels brought world news, relayed out of the United States. And often American ships took official despatches from Australia home to London.

Australian colonial crews began a tentative entry into the whaling and sealing industries. Soon they were in conflict with the Americans. One confrontation involved an American sea captain, Amasa Delano, who had sailed three times around the world. Delano reached Kent's Bay on Furneaux's Island in Bass Strait in 1804 with two ships, the *Pilgrim* and the *Perseverance*. He found a sloop already there. She was the *Surprize,* owned by Messrs Kable and Underwood of Sydney and commanded by Joseph Murrell.

According to Captain Murrell, the Americans captured him at four in the morning. They beat him with clubs and took him down to the beach where he was kept naked for almost one hour. The Americans caught another of his crew, tied both men to a tree and gave them several dozen lashes with a rope's end. 'A Sandwich Island savage' battered Murrell about the head and arms with a club. Amasa Delano alleged afterwards that Murrell and his men had been frightening off their seals and that Murrell had led an attack on the Americans, armed with a cutlass.

Governor King had other reasons to dislike Captain Amasa Delano. The American had assisted a disabled British vessel but had charged an extortionate fee. When Delano eventually sailed away from Australia he took with him 17 escaped convicts.

One of Captain Delano's descendants was to become the longest-serving president of the United States, President Franklin Delano Roosevelt, a somewhat quieter man.

In early times the convict port of Sydney was a wretched place. Chain gangs slaved on public and private projects, their overseers brutally forcing the pace. Ferocious floggings for relatively minor offences were routine. Unfortunates received as many as 1000 lashes across their bared backs. Public executions were humane by comparison.

Eye-witness accounts of the Sydney convict settlement were taken back to the United States by American seamen. Its notoriety spread.

Captain Percival of the American ship, *Charles*, of Boston, beached his vessel in 1803 in Kent's Bay on Furneaux's Island to careen its hull. The cargo unloaded from his ship was stacked on the beach when along came the *Edwin*, a sealing vessel out of Sydney. Captain Percival thought he saw the Sydney men eyeing his cargo as if planning to steal it. He marooned seven of the Sydney sealers on a small island without water. To be fair to Captain Percival you must be informed that he released his prisoners before they died but they were in bruised and battered shape.

The skins of fur seals were worth one guinea a piece. In the early nineteenth century that was big money.. The competitive Americans were not willing to share their bonanza meekly.

Seal hunters were a tough lot. They worked along the beaches and the rocks among the defenceless lumbering seal herds, clubbing them systematically to death at the rate of hundreds by the day. Though enriching their employers, their bloody slaughtering brutalised those who were wielding crimson-stained clubs.

Fanning & Company of New York obtained a copy of Vancouver's journal, 'Voyages', in which he mentioned the presence of seals on the south-west coast of New Holland. The company decided in 1803 to send one of its ships to Australia on a voyage of investigation, sealing and trading. The *Union*, a brig of 120 tons and commanded by Captain Isaac Pendleton, set out for the south seas via the Cape of Good Hope. Pendleton had instructions to use his own judgement after his arrival at King George's Sound in south-west Australia but he was to leave a letter in a corked bottle on the seal island mentioned by Vancouver in his journal. His letter would advise the masters of other company ships likely to pass that way later of any commercial potential he had discovered.

Captain Pendleton found only 30 seals on Vancouver's island. He sailed further east, running before a gale and rough seas in the Great Australian Bight until reaching Kangaroo Island off the South Australian coast. There he saw more seals than he could count.

The *Union* remained anchored in sheltered waters off Kangaroo Island for the rest of the season. Crewmen battered their way through the placid seal colonies until exhaustion or darkness every day brought an end to their grisly work. The crew of the *Union* clubbed and skinned a total of 14 000 seals in a matter of weeks. Thousands more remained on beaches now stinking with carcasses and blackened by gore.

Captain Pendleton needed another vessel to carry away his fur skins. He had his men chop down suitable trees in the surrounding forests, from which carpenters cut and dressed timber for the task. They built a schooner of 40 tons and named her the *Independence.*

Governor King fretted when he learned from the Americans that they had been sealing in uncontrolled coastal territory and had built a ship. But times were tough and King needed Captain Pendleton's assistance. Supplies had to be sent urgently to Norfolk Island, the Pacific outpost on which the worst desperadoes of the Australian colony were languishing. He hired the *Union* to do the job.

Afterwards Governor King learned that Pendleton overcame a shortage of crew for his two ships by taking men from Norfolk

Island without official permission.

Unluckily for Captain Pendleton he met a former convict, Simeon Lord, who had become a merchant in Sydney. Lord saw an opportunity to evade the British Government's ban on trade with China other than through the East India Company. He made a deal with Pendleton to pick up a cargo of sandalwood in Fiji and take it for him to China in his American vessel. Technically this would not be a breach of British law if the arrangements were handled shrewdly. The outrageous monopoly enjoyed by the East India Company through British legislation disadvantaged other British traders but once cargoes were loaded into American vessels the game had different rules.

Simeon Lord had been convicted at Manchester Quarter Sessions in 1790 of stealing several rolls of cloth and had been transported to Australia for seven years hard labour. He had arrived in Sydney in July 1791 at the age of 20, fair-haired, handsome, intelligent and unscrupulous. He was assigned to Captain Thomas Rowley, one of a group of army officers who were buying cargoes direct from ships' captains, and became so useful he was freed. Lord became a public auctioneer and from 1793 began obtaining land grants. He built a warehouse beside the Sydney docks and in 1803 owned a mansion close to his warehouse. It had servants' quarters, extensive cellars and an auction room.

Captain Pendleton stored his 14 000 seal skins in Simeon Lord's warehouse in Sydney. He sent his new schooner *Independence,* back to southern Australia for another cargo of seal skins and took the *Union* to Fiji to pick up Lord's consignment of sandalwood for China. Pendleton calculated that by the time he returned from China his sealing party would have finished its work. His two ships would then leave Australia, laden with furs, a rich return for the trust Fanning & Company had placed in him.

Some romantic person had misnamed the Friendly Islands. This name was marked invitingly on the maps of that era and misled seamen visiting that part of the Pacific for the first time.

It was well enough known that fierce savages inhabited many of the island groups of the Pacific. Maoris had killed some of Abel Tasman's men in New Zealand, Captain James Cook had been murdered by the Polynesians of the Hawaiian Islands. Every mariner knew that the Portuguese discoverer, Magellan, had been done to death in the Philippines.

Pendleton anchored the *Union* off Tongataboo (probably Tongatapu). He decided he would go ashore and engage one of the friendly local people as an interpreter. He took with him Simeon Lord's agent, a Mr Boston, and an unsuspecting boat's crew.

Pendleton and his men disappeared inland, walking with confidence as if still on Kangaroo Island off South Australia where the Aborigines and seals had been so peaceful.

Natives' canoes came out from the shore and surrounded the *Union*. The Chief Mate, Daniel Wright, who had been left in command of the ship, placed the remainder of his crew on armed alert and kept the canoes at a distance. The big frizzy-haired Polynesians made welcoming gestures to Wright, smiling with teeth sharpened to points. Wearing little else but shark-teeth necklaces and shell armlets, they gestured to Wright that he should send a second shore party to the beach. Wright ordered his men to fire their guns and frightened them off.

After a while another canoe came paddling out from shore and in its bows stood a white woman. The islanders were using her as a decoy.

When the canoe was closer the woman screamed a warning, struggled free, and jumped overboard. The crew of the *Union* fired another volley of musketry to hold back the islanders as the woman began swimming. Soon she was alongside and was dragged on board.

She told Wright what he had already guessed – that Captain Pendleton and all his men had been murdered. Wright abandoned the plan to pick up a cargo of sandalwood for China and returned to Sydney.

The fate of Captain Pendleton and his men caused a sensation in the colony. Equally as terrible was the story of the white woman, Elizabeth Morey. She was a survivor from the American ship, *Duke of Portland*, which had made the mistake of visiting the same island some months earlier (*Sydney Gazette*, 28 October 1804). The islanders had killed the captain of the *Duke of Portland* and most of his crew but had spared Elizabeth Morey, her native servant, four youths and an old man. Later the youths retook the ship and departed. The old man was killed, leaving Elizabeth Morey alone among the islanders.

The merchant, Simeon Lord, was more interested in lost business than in stories of lost lives. He went after the hesitant Daniel Wright and began harassing him to fulfil the sandalwood contract to which the late Captain Pendleton had agreed. He demanded that Wright return to the islands forthwith, pick up the cargo and take it to China.

Displaying poor seamanship as well as poor judgement Wright allowed the *Union* to be caught in a squall in narrow waters amid the islands of Fiji. At the best of times the *Union* was a clumsy vessel, slow to respond to the helm and requiring a lot of sea room in which to manoeuvre. The brig could not sail out of trouble and was cast up onto a reef. All hands perished, either from drowning, or later at the hands of the islanders.

Eventually news of this fresh disaster reached Sydney (*Sydney Gazette*, 28 April 1805). The opportunist, Simeon Lord, immediately chartered another vessel, and sailed to the sealing island where Pendleton's men were encamped. He told them a plausible story and took possession of the 60 000 fur skins they had accumulated by prodigious labour with clubs and knives.

Lord carried the skins back to Sydney, adding them to the 14 000 which Pendleton had placed earlier in his warehouse. He arranged for the grand total of 74 000 sealskins to be sent to China and sold although they were legally the property of Fanning & Company of New York. Lord used the money from the sale to buy Chinese goods. He resold these in the United States, thereby increasing his unlawful gains.

Captain Pendleton's sealing party were never to give evidence against Lord. They left the sealing area to sail to Sydney in their home-made ship but failed to arrive. It was assumed in Sydney that the schooner foundered in the rough seas of Bass Strait. For Lord theirs was a convenient disappearance.

Of all the crew of the *Union*, who left New York in 1803 for a voyage of discovery and trade in Australian waters, not one survived.

Simeon Lord continued to prosper. In 1807, one of his ships brought convicts from England to Sydney, only 16 years after he had made the same voyage in chains. A few years later, Lord became a magistrate – to the fury of the free society of Sydney. He was appointed by Governor Macquarie who believed that once a man had served his sentence his past should be forgiven and forgotten. Fanning & Company of New York must have felt less benign towards him.

Lord became a manufacturer, using convict labour and in 1817 was one of 13 capitalists who put up the money for the establishment of the new Bank of New South Wales. His four sons became worthy members of parliament and his two daughters married well. Lord died rich in 1840, respected and able to afford scruples. To the day he died he had a soft spot for Americans.

The American pioneers of the whaling and sealing industries strongly influenced the Australian colonies. Except for the French exploring expeditions of the era, the visits of the American adventurers represented the first impact of the outside world on the Australian settlements.

Their impact on the whale and seal population of the southern seas was something else. Within a short time the Governor at Hobart could sleep undisturbed at night in his official residence on the banks of the Derwent River. Whales had sported and splashed in the river every season for thousands of years but now the Derwent had become empty of their presence.

Up to 1833, whale oil and whalebone – and a diminishing quantity of sealskins – formed half of Australia's total exports;

but it was a temporary trade with no thought for conservation. The seal herds of the southern coastline of Australia and adjacent islands had existed in vast numbers throughout the ages, but went the way of the bison of the American prairies and with much the same speed. Their commercial slaughtering was so intensive that fur seals almost became extinct in Australian waters during the first half of the nineteenth century.

To continue the industry, American sealers had to hunt further afield, as far south as Heard Island in the Antarctic.

In 1829, the British Government, becoming uneasy about American and French ships prowling the oceans around the Australian continent, decided to claim total ownership. It sent Captain Charles Fremantle to establish a new settlement at King George's Sound on the west coast of Australia and to claim, in the name of the British Crown, all of the country stretching across to Sydney in the east, over 3 000 kilometres distant.

American Rebels
In the early 1800s, colonists in Canada were demanding severance from the British Empire. A 'Declaration of the Reformers' was published in Toronto and closely resembles the American Declaration of Independence.

Because of this unrest on the other side of the Pacific, Australia was to receive a unique shipment of convicts. They were United States citizens.

The British put down the first Canadian rebellion of 1837, capturing many who had taken up arms against the Crown. They hanged some for treason. Hundreds of other rebels escaped across the St Lawrence River and into the United States including the two leaders, Lyon Mackenzie and the French Canadian, Louis Papineau.

The Canadian political refugees aroused excitement and sympathy when their story became known in northern United States. A news journal in the border town of Buffalo published fiery editorials proposing an American invasion of Canada to free her from British tyranny. In Michigan, eager young

Americans began drilling for an expeditionary force. Associations to work for American assistance for the Canadian rebels were formed in Cleveland, Cincinnati, Rochester, Detroit, Buffalo and Watertown. In Detroit, arms and ammunition, including cannon, were stolen from the public arsenals to equip an invasion army. Ships in US ports were being equipped for war.

The President of the United States, Martin van Buren, issued a proclamation expressing his regret that Americans were involving themselves in the Canadian uprising. The US Congress passed an Act to enable government seizure of any American vessel, arms or ammunition intended for any unauthorised military adventure into Canada. This official disapproval went unheeded in the northern regions of the United States where preparations for an invasion were far advanced.

In the second stage of the Canadian rebellion, armed American volunteers crossed the border and in November 1838 fought the British at the battle of Prescott. They were defeated. Once more the British arrested hundreds of rebels and this time they included American citizens. The British identified ringleaders among the prisoners-of-war and executed them. Some were Americans.

The Lieutenant Governor of Upper Canada was the infamous Sir George Arthur who had been commandant of a convict settlement in Tasmania eleven years earlier. Arthur discussed with his executive council what should be done with the rebels still in custody. He suggested that the council give free pardons to those whose youth and inexperience lessened their guilt. In case this clemency hinted that Arthur was becoming soft in his old age he also recommended that the other prisoners be transported to the Australian penal settlements that he remembered so vividly and to whose terrible record he had contributed.

Seventy-eight United States citizens who had been sentenced to death for 'piratical invasion of Upper Canada' had their sentences commuted to transportation. They joined French Canadians being loaded into the British ship, HMS Buffalo, in the St Lawrence River, and sailed for Australia on 28 September 1839.

During the voyage informers betrayed some of the American captives who had been plotting to take the vessel. Captain J.V. Wood tightened discipline. Thereafter the voyage became uncomfortable for all.

On 14 February 1840, HMS Buffalo arrived at Hobart where the Americans were landed. The French Canadian prisoners were taken on to the penal settlement in Sydney.

The legality of transporting United States nationals as convicts from one British colony to another was questionable. An attorney-general in Tasmania, Edward McDowell, expressed his opinion that the Americans were being held without lawful authority, but made no attempt to have this view tested officially.

The Lieutenant Governor of Van Diemen's Land, Sir John Franklin, (the Arctic explorer) decided that as the Americans were political prisoners they would be kept out of the convict barracks. Franklin also obtained official approval to release the Americans after they had done two years of hard labour on the roads. All served much longer. Officialdom in Australia had a habit of forgetting promises to convicts, no matter what their crimes or their nationality.

A controversy was raging in the United States and petitions were presented to Congress to secure the release of the Americans. The matter was debated in the Senate in 1841. Senator Ferris, of New York, said that the prisoners had been motivated by love of liberty and were national heroes. John Quincy Adams, a senator from Massachusetts, had a different point of view. He said that the prisoners in Van Diemen's Land were there because they had participated in the Canadian Rebellion, and in defiance of an earlier proclamation by the President of the United States, forbidding such action. They had invaded another country, against the laws of their own country. When captured, they had been mercifully transported

– according to Adams – instead of being executed as they might legally have been.

It was not until 1844 that the British Government at last granted free pardons to the French Canadian convicts in New South Wales and to the American and Canadian prisoners in Van Diemen's Land. By then a few had died. Two others had escaped in American ships.

One American escapee, James Wait, published in Buffalo in 1843 an account of his sufferings. His book had a lengthy title – *Van Diemen's Land, Written During Four Years Imprisonment for Political Offences Committed in Upper Canada.* Copies went into the Canadian Archives in Ottawa. Another, Stephen Wright, described Sir George Arthur in his book, *Narrative and Recollections during a Three Years' Captivity*, as 'that cold-blooded villain who was the bloody Robespierre of the Canadian revolution'. Wright said of Arthur, 'His eye gleamed from beneath its heavy brush with the ferocity of a bloodhound breaking cover'. He claimed that in Van Diemen's Land, a clergyman who was requested to preach a funeral service upon the death of a prisoner, declined by saying that convicts had no souls. He hoped he would not be insulted again by so impertinent a request.

When the American Civil War began in 1861 public opinion in Australia was sharply divided. Some supported the northerners because of their stand against slavery. Other Australians were inclined to sympathise with the underdogs in any conflict and hoped that the Confederates would win. Americans in Australia, many of them left over from the goldrush, took sides according to their native loyalties.

One day in January 1865 the Confederate raiding vessel, *Shenandoah*, entered Port Phillip, Melbourne. Her officers and crew needed supplies, rest and recreation after months of hunting Union ships across the Indian ocean.

The *Shenandoah* was a steamer of 790 tons, British-built on the Clyde in 1863. She was also rigged as a full clipper sailing ship. When under sail, her screw could be lifted out of the water and with all canvas set could do 17 knots, more than double her speed as a steamer. The *Shenandoah* normally had a crew of 140 but when she reached Melbourne this number was well down. The Captain of the *Shenandoah* was James Waddell, a dashing young officer from North Carolina who limped slightly from a dueling wound. One of his junior officers was Third Lieutenant Sydney Smith Lee, a nephew of General Robert E. Lee, the Confederate Commander-in-Chief.

The *Shenandoah* dropped anchor in Port Phillip a little before sunset. Crowds went out in steamboats to welcome the American rebels. They cheered the crew, tossed local newspapers on board and shouted greetings. Later the Melbourne newspaper, *The Age*, reported sardonically that as soon as the *Shenandoah* had entered Melbourne alarm was shown by several American ships in port. All of them ran up their national colours, except for one panicked Yankee who hoisted a strange bit of bunting afterwards described as the Ionian flag.

Victoria's Minister for Justice, Archibald Michie, told the Governor, Sir Charles Darling, that the *Shenandoah* had captured and burned eleven Union merchantmen in three months before arriving in Melbourne. Prisoners taken had included several women.

Members of Melbourne's American community held agitated meetings in the Criterion Hotel. Supporters of the Northerners in the Civil War claimed that the *Shenandoah* was no better than a private vessel and that James Waddell was a buccaneer who should be arrested forthwith. The Confederate faction said the captain and crew of the *Shenandoah* were gallant war heroes. The Melbourne *Age* newspaper ran stories comparing the recent deeds of Captain Waddell of the *Shenandoah* with the swashbuckling feats of Sir Francis Drake and Sir Walter Raleigh on the Spanish Main.

A shore party from the *Shenandoah* marched down Collins Street to the lusty strains of 'The Bonny Blue Flag', the national anthem of the Southern States. A number of young women on the sidewalks were overcome by the glamour of it all and swooned. The people of Melbourne arranged social functions and excursions for Waddell and his men. Confederate sympathisers took them to meet other Confederate sympathisers at the goldfields town of Ballarat.

Captain Waddell had released his prisoners when he reached Melbourne. He was praised for his chivalrous treatment of the women he had captured. Waddell had given them the best cabin in his ship.

One of these women showed a lack of gratitude by complaining to the United States consul in Melbourne that Captain Waddell had not permitted her to take any item of her luggage off the ship, *Dephine*, when it was captured and sunk. She had tried to claim books that had been brought across to the *Shenandoah* from the *Dephine*. A junior officer of the Confederate crew, Lieutenant Whittel, had taken her copy of *Uncle Tom's Cabin*, held it up between his thumb and forefinger and had dropped it contemptuously into the ocean.

The American Consul in Melbourne was William Blanchard. As soon as the *Shenandoah* arrived he asked port authorities to seize the *Shenandoah* as a pirate vessel. They told him that Australian colonists were neutral in the affairs of the American Civil War. The raider and its crew were entitled to the same regulated liberties available to ships and crews from any other foreign nation.

Goodwill between Captain Waddell and the colonial administrators in Melbourne began to wear thin. In the first instance, Waddell complained that Melbourne police were not helping him to find and arrest a number of deserters from the *Shenandoah* who had decided that for them the Civil War had ended. On the other hand, Waddell's attempts to recruit additional crew for the *Shenandoah* in Melbourne had become public knowledge and Governor Darling told him that this was a breach of neutrality and a strain on friendship.

The *Shenandoah* had been hauled up onto a slipway for careening and repairs. After months at sea her underwater hull was thick with marine growth and this had been slowing her down. Now it was being scraped off. Following arguments between Captain Waddell and the Melbourne authorities, however, Governor Darling issued an Order that repair work on the *Shenandoah* be suspended.

The *Shenandoah* was sitting helplessly in its cradle on the slipway like a trussed duck when a force of 50 policemen, armed with carbines, arrived to enforce the Governor's decision. A shore battery tried to train its guns on the vessel but intervening high ground prevented this.

The police guard around the *Shenandoah* deterred Northerners in the American community from attacking the ship, but Mr Blanchard, the United States Consul, had not given up. He went to the Crown Solicitor, Mr H.F. Gurner, and demanded that the port authorities seize and search the *Shenandoah*. Mr Gurner replied that the matter was not Crown Law business. Blanchard then went to the Attorney-General, Mr Higinbotham, who passed him on to a police magistrate, Mr E Sturt, who in turn suggested that Mr Blanchard should ask the Water Police if they would help him. He was introduced quickly around and left on his own like a debt collector in a Jerusalem market.

The exasperated consul wrote an official report to Washington. This document was to become important evidence later at an international inquiry.

Governor Darling realised that the best solution to problems being created by the presence of the *Shenandoah* would be the ship's earliest possible departure. He cancelled his Order of Restraint, withdrew his cordon of police and permitted completion of repairs to the ship. Additional stores were loaded, the ship was re-launched, and on Saturday, 18 February 1865, the raider put to sea, ready to fight again.

On his way out of Melbourne, Captain Waddell fired a few blank rounds from his guns in defiance of the few who had been unfriendly, and in farewell salute to the many citizens of the colony of Victoria who had given his officers and crew a warm welcome. William Temple, a British seaman who served in *Shenandoah* later wrote the following revealing account:

We were well received by all the authorities and people at Melbourne. All the officials and most of the leading inhabitants of the place visited the *Shenandoah* and were very warm in their congratulations and well wishes to us. The Governor of Melbourne visited Captain Waddell and was privately entertained by Captain Waddell on board the *Shenandoah*. There were 8 000 visitors came on board to see us in one day. All the Government officials were on board to see us and most of them were entertained on board, either by the Captain or his officers. The Government officials in Melbourne gave an elegant entertainment to Captain Waddell and his officers during his stay there; it was given at their club room in Melbourne. Every facility was afforded to us, both by the officials and people of Melbourne to make our repairs and to procure our supplies; indeed everything she wanted. One very warm friend was a former United States Consul in Melbourne. A dinner was given to the officers of the *Shenandoah* at a place called Ballarat in the country. They were received at the station by some 2 000 people who cheered them as they passed.

The English Government engineer was on board our ship while we were undergoing our repairs three or four times a day, and certainly assisted them with his opinions and advice, if he did not superintend our repairs.

We left Melbourne on the 18th day of February. When we left we had from 50 to 60 persons on board as stowaways; among them was Captain Blacker, who commanded the English steamer, *Saxonia*. It was known to the officers on board at the time we sailed that most of these men were on board. All these persons so stowed away on board were British subjects, and were enlisted or enrolled upon the ship's books as officers or men within 12 hours from the time we left our anchorage and while we were within sight of land. Their names are mentioned in the list annexed hereto, and comprise all those set down in said list as shipping at Melbourne.

(The list contained the names of 42 men who had joined the *Shenandoah* in Melbourne.)

After leaving Melbourne the *Shenandoah* wreaked havoc among the American whaling fleet in the North Pacific. Before the end of the war the raider had sunk or captured 38 vessels.

Following the American Civil War the United States Government claimed damages of $US19,077,798 against Great Britain for involvement in some aspects of the recent hostilities. Of this amount $US6,303,039 related to the release of the *Shenandoah* from Melbourne and the damage that the raider subsequently caused to shipping. An international jury sat in Geneva in 1872 and decided by three votes to two that Great Britain was responsible for the negligence of Victoria, a British colony, in allowing *Shenandoah* to put to sea, and should be called upon to pay compensation for the belligerent acts that Captain Waddell committed after leaving Melbourne. The British Government paid $US3,875,000 to the United States in compensation for the damage that the *Shenandoah* had done.

Confederate raiders, including the *Shenandoah*, destroyed or captured more than 250 ocean-going Union vessels during the American Civil War. At least 700 other Union ships were transferred to foreign registry, mainly British, to avoid capture or increased insurance rates. The Confederate raiders dealt a shattering blow to the United States merchant marine from which it did not recover for at least 80 years.

The *Shenandoah* later was sold and became a merchant vessel trading in China. Captain Waddell went back to sea in peacetime. He died at Annapolis in the United States in 1886.

2 Gold Rush

Less than two years after the United States annexed the Mexican province of California, gold was discovered there. The exciting news spread across the Pacific and reached Australia. Between 1848 and 1851 an estimated 7 000 Australians and New Zealanders departed for the Californian goldfields. Their voyage across the Pacific took only about 70 days. Australia was much closer in travelling time to California than was the east coast of America overland or around the Horn.

From Australia to California

Australia's bad reputation as a British penal settlement was widely known. Californians looked at all new arrivals from Australia with suspicion. In fact, only a small percentage were former British convicts, but they were too many. (According to Charles Bateson's check of records of 2 123 arrivals from Sydney only 279 were known to have been convicts.)

A citizens' committee in San Francisco formed a vigilante force. They lynched an ex-convict from Sydney, John Jenkins, for alleged theft. He was the first.

Another former convict from Sydney, James Stuart, had become an outlaw in California. Stuart had been convicted of forgery in England at the age of 16 but in California he turned to crimes of violence. He murdered Charles Moore, Sheriff of Yuba County, and robbed the customs house at Monterey. When captured he confessed to numerous other murders and robberies. A large crowd, including 500 vigilantes, took Stuart to the Market Street wharf in San Francisco, put a noose about his neck and suspended him from a loading derrick.

According to the vigilantes, Stuart's last words were: 'I die resigned – my sentence is just'. It was an unlikely story but was given to those people in San Francisco who were opposed to the vigilantes taking the law into their own hands.

Another ex-convict from Sydney, Sam Whittaker, and a companion, Bob Mackenzie, fell into the hands of vigilantes but were rescued by law authorities. The vigilantes were not to be thwarted and stormed the jail-house to recapture both men. Within minutes they had hanged them in public, this time watched by a crowd of 15 000 men, women and children. Lynching was becoming a popular spectator event in San Francisco.

It disillusioned those in Australia who had nurtured romantic notions about American democracy. The *Sydney Morning Herald* and other Australian newspapers reported full details. They described the vigilantes as being a scandal to justice and to civilisation. (The vigilantes cross-examined 89 suspected criminals in unofficial public courts, hanged four, whipped one, deported 14, ordered 14 others to leave town, handed 15 to legal authorities and discharged 41.)

Californian authorities introduced immigration restrictions against undesirables from Australia. When this became known in Australia, public indignation was intense. The Melbourne newspaper, *The Age*, led the attack with a stinging editorial, advocating similar immigration laws in Australia to keep out undesirable Californians. When the Australian gold rush started soon afterwards and Californian miners began arriving, Henry Parkes, editor of *The Empire*, wrote in his newspaper, 'let no door be opened to receive bloodstained wretches'.

The exchange of hard-bitten citizens across the Pacific between Australia and California included Irish rebels who had been transported to Australia for treason against Britain. Californians gave them a better reception than other 'Sydney Ducks'. One of them, Thomas Francis Meagher, became an American citizen. He fought for the Union in the Civil War as a brigadier general in command of the Irish Brigade. After the

Americans at McIvor diggings, Victoria, 1859.

war, President Andrew Jackson appointed Meagher Governor of Montana Territory.

Americans and the Australian Rush

Australians returning from the Californian goldfields in 1851 included Edward Hammond Hargraves and Jim Esmond. They had been struck by the similarities between gold bearing country in California and regions of Australia with which they were familiar. As soon as they arrived home both men began prospecting, using their American expertise. Hargraves found gold at Lewis Ponds Creek in New South Wales. Jim Esmond made a much richer find at Clunes in Victoria. And so began the Australian gold rush.

It transformed Melbourne into a roaring boom town. Its original buildings became lost in a great surrounding encampment of tents and shacks. Melbourne became a city of murder and robbery by night or by day, a city of tumult, danger and vice. It had 100 brothels. Family men who had emigrated from Britain took one look at Melbourne and hurried their families back on board ship. Women and children, landed too soon in Melbourne by their impatient menfolk, often had to sleep on bare ground because of a shortage of beds. In dry weather, the town was swept by clouds of dust; when it rained Melbourne was deep in mud.

A contemporary writer gave this eyewitness account of the scene at one of the city's banks:

> Miners in blue woollen frocks and corduroy and with a fagged and wretched appearance, were getting their small bags of gold changed into cash. One fellow rubbed his face as we stood by and as he had been previously putting his hand into the gold dust one side of his face appeared perfectly gilt.

A report of a Melbourne wedding of that time stated that the bride was drunk and fraternising with the populace and was seen leaning, with bottle in hand, from her carriage window.

It is fairly clear that some Melbourne people lacked style.

Lord Robert Cecil, who was to become Prime Minister of Great Britain, went to the Australian goldfields at the age of twenty-two. His diary includes a graphic description of a Californian gold prospector who travelled with him to the Victorian gold diggings in a springcart:

> He was a coarse hideous dirty looking man, without any attempt at ornament or even neatness in his dress; yet he wore in his ears a pair of ear-rings about the size and shape of a wedding ring. He wore a pair of pistols in his belt, and the words, 'put a bullet through his brain' were continually in his mouth . . . '

The gold rush gathered pace. Freed convicts headed for the goldfields with their former prison guards. American adventurers, British deserters, Canadians, Irish, Germans and native-born colonial Australians joined them. Riff-raff and good citizens mixed. Services broke down as storekeepers, clerks, bush workers, civil servants, policemen and ships' crews left

Waterfall of the American Creek, NSW. The name was given by the American gold seekers and the date of the drawing is December 5 1859.

their jobs, believing stories that gold nuggets could be picked up in handfuls in the new finds.

A government official described how hundreds of desperate men tried to defend as much ground as they could hold until surveyors arrived to peg out their claims and make them legal. They formed a seething carpet of humanity, lying on their backs all over the paddocks throughout the day. Their legs and arms were outstretched to hold as wide a section as possible. Many, according to the eyewitness, were clutching a pistol in one hand and a knife in the other.

The miners saw gold as a gift from nature to any person who could locate it and who was strong enough to keep it. This sometimes meant that successful miners had to fight off newcomers. Gold-crazed men went crawling into tunnels being dug by others to seize their gold as it loosened from the earth.

The National Library in Canberra records that a Kentuckian found such a thief at the bottom of a shaft he had dug, scurrying about like a rat. Intent on picking up small nuggets and specks of gold, he was unresponsive to all warnings to stop. The American miner applied law of ownership by dropping a heavy piece of quartz eight feet down the shaft onto the man's head, knocking him unconscious. Miners dragged the thief to the surface, emptied his pockets, and threw him into a creek to return him to his senses.

Between August and December in 1851, more than 21 000 ounces of gold reached Melbourne from the new Victorian diggings. The fabulous 'Welcome Stranger' nugget found at Ballarat in Victoria weighed 2 284 ounces. Holtermann's nugget uncovered later at Hill End in New South Wales weighed 7 560 ounces.

An American businessman, George Train, found the road to the Victorian mines strewn with broken carts, old drays, and with dead bullocks and horses lying in all stages of decay, and 'everything that was sickening to the sight'. Bullock wagons, creaking and groaning along the rough tracks, were carrying freight at £150 a ton. Train wrote:

> I suppose that in no place in the world is there such cruelty to animals as here. The poor bullocks in their iron-bowed yokes being the great sufferers. The driver's whip is as long as a fishing pole and the crack of it as loud as a pistol shot.

Throughout every night, miners kept up a desultory fire with their weapons to warn ill-disposed persons that they were armed. The danger of being hit by stray bullets was considerable. Train observed: 'The moment the sun goes down you have a perfect bedlam in the camp – screeching, swearing and singing, pistol shots and barking dogs all mingled together'. About 80 000 people were living in tents and shanties on the goldfields. Many of them regularly became high on 'New England champagne', a potent aerated beverage introduced by American miners and which sometimes exploded in its bottles like a bomb.

George Francis Train, merchant, traveller, sharp observer and revolutionary-republican, arrived in Melbourne in May

George Francis Train.

1853, aged 24, in his company's ship, *Bavaria*, at the peak of the gold rush and at a time when merchants were making a pile of money. Train had thrust his way into the business firm of a relative, Colonel Enoch Train of Boston. He had been sent to Melbourne to establish a new branch of the company to be known as Caldwell, Train and Company.

Hundreds of ships were anchored in the port of Melbourne, most of them waiting to be unloaded. Train deplored the slow, antiquated lighterage system and the absence of wharves. He saw many opportunities as he walked around the raw city, impeccably dressed, carrying a cane and with a veil wrapped around his face to shut out some of the dust. Other American businessmen told him they were making profits of up to 200 percent.

Train built a new office, and a warehouse with iron window shutters for security. He spent much of his time in the Criterion Hotel in Collins Street which had become a favourite meeting place for Yankees. The Criterion Hotel was a marvel for a frontier town. It had a grand and lofty hall of noble dimensions and was most elegantly fitted out as a billiard saloon. It possessed other refinements, including an excellent barbershop, a bath house with hot or cold vapour or shower baths, and a theatre to hold 500 people. The dining room had a splendid reputation; the hotel's cellars were stocked with fine wines. In the public bar, the American barmen were as skilful as jugglers, pouring beer into glasses at great speed, whipping them out along the bar to customers with a professional flourish and without spilling a drop, except now and then.

The American proprietor, Sam Moss, was intent on introducing to Melbourne a standard of quality and service not previously known there. All Melbourne people of prominence and power, from the Governor down, patronised the Criterion. Reports say that some gentlemen of Melbourne were there before breakfast for 'phlegm-cutters'. The Criterion had a skylight through which was thrust a flagpole every 4 July, proudly bearing the Stars and Stripes. The sign across the front entrance to the hotel proclaimed 'Ice, Ice, Ice'.

The hotel's American customers were a striking lot with broad-brimmed hats, sashes around their waists, and bell-bottomed trousers. Their Uncle Sam beards wagged non-stop as they preached about profits and progress and American expansion – or 'spread-eagleism', as they called it.

In one of his letters home from Melbourne, Train wrote:

> You will be surprised to see how fast this place is becoming Americanised. Go where you will . . . and you can but note some indication of the indomitable energy of our people . . . The true American defies competition and laughs sneeringly at impossibilities. He don't believe in the word, and is prepared to show how meaningless it is.

The American arrivals had brought with them to Australia new tools for mining. They had American axes and picks and shovels not available before in Australia. American merchants were importing alarm clocks and rocking chairs, iron stoves and bacon and flour. The first Boston water cart to lay the dust of Melbourne's streets was the start of the city's municipal services. It was a barrel-like arrangement and attracted great attention the first day it went to work. One man leaped up onto the cart to inform the driver that the thing was full of holes and leaking. Shopkeepers who subscribed to the American watering service had the dust laid in the streets outside their premises several times a day. Those who did not contribute soon learned that the water could be turned off as it passed their door.

Americans established the Melbourne fire brigade on an efficient basis following a succession of fires through the tent town, that had spread to the newer, more solid buildings. The Americans financed the brigade by raising $US16,000 within a few hours one morning amid the ashes of an overnight disaster.

Americans were supplying Melbourne with fresh fish caught along the coast; others were cutting firewood for the city on speculation and making a good business of it. One hundred imported New York buggies carried their new owners through Melbourne streets. Americans won the contract to build the Hobson Bay Railroad Pier for Port Melbourne. An American engineer, Sam McGowan, built the first telegraph line in Australia to flash news of approaching ships from the entrance of the port to the centre of the city. (McGowan was a pupil of Samuel Morse. He emigrated to Australia in 1853.)

The Victorian Government appointed McGowan Superintendent of an Electric Telegraph Department. By 1857, Melbourne was linked by telegraph to main country centres and interstate to Sydney and Adelaide. McGowan remained head of the service until his death in 1887.

Train helped to establish Melbourne's stock exchange in temporary premises, contributing the first membership fee of three guineas and urging other businessmen to join. Somebody proposed that a statue of Queen Victoria be erected outside the stock exchange. Train suggested that a statue of George Washington also be placed there.

By 1 January 1854, George Francis Train was depressed. He was thinking of his friends at home in Boston, celebrating the new year in the white snows of mid-winter. He wrote:

> Here I am *sans* ice, *sans* fruit, *sans* everything but the blues, the Australian indigo blues! Who can help it when suffocating with heat, eaten up with flies, and choking with dust. Twenty-five cents for a little dried up peach, $2 for a quart of cherries, 50 cents for a seed cucumber . . . Give me the rainy season with all its mud and dampness rather than this pestilential fiery scorching dust-choking sirocco which almost drives me mad. The country far and wide is parched with the intense heat and the few cattle are dying for food and water.

By that time Train had come to believe that he was living in a human rubbish dump, full of the worst of humanity from

Newgate and other British prisons. He had fallen into the habit of glumly looking at the people he passed during his daily walks, wondering who was a burglar, forger, or murderer. He recorded how two former convicts were captured after having killed between 15 and 20 people. During Train's first five months in Melbourne eight or nine public hangings had been watched by thousands 'of the lower orders' of the population. Those executed included three of a gang of bandits who had ambushed a gold convoy and shot the escorting policemen off their horses. The following day, Train was disgusted to see the blue-faced, pop-eyed corpse of one of the hanged bandits on exhibition in the window of a drinking saloon. It had been decorated with flowers and ribbons.

Train was confident that Melbourne would become a great city, although situated so far out of the way. He wrote:

> All we need is a little energy and a good deal of money to make the wheel turn rapidly. We must introduce a sprinkling of Yankeeism here and show the residents the meaning of despatch.

Train conferred with another American, Freeman Cobb, of the American express agents, Adams and Company. As a result of this conference there was formed one of the greatest coach companies the world ever saw. The first four drivers of the Cobb & Co. stage coaches were Americans John Peck, James Swanton, Antony Black and John Lamber. They opened a fast parcel delivery and passenger service between Melbourne and the goldfields, driving their horses through the dust and ruts and heat in the best style of Wells Fargo to deliver the mails in quick time. Cobb & Co. became so successful that at the peak of its operations throughout eastern Australia it was harnessing 6 000 horses every day. Its coaches were travelling a total of 28 000 miles each week. They were Concords from the United States. The drivers, like those driving similar Concords in the American West of the same period, were armed against holdup men

Cobb & Co. coach crossing a flooded river in NSW.

after mail and gold consignments. Bushranger gangs frequently lay in wait outside towns. It was a brave driver who tried to race his horses through their gunfire. Sometimes he became a dead driver.

One bandit was Frank Gardiner, whose gang of seven included the infamous but handsome Ben Hall, and the aboriginal renegade, Johnny Gilbert. The gang ambushed a Cobb & Co. coach and overturned it among boulders. They shot two of the police escort during the gunfight and got away with 2 715 ounces of gold, and a fortune in bank notes.

Gardiner and his men did not wear body armour and helmets like the bushranger, Ned Kelly, of a later era. They moved fast and light. Fate overtook them one by one. Some were caught and hanged. Police surrounded and shot Johnny Gilbert and Ben Hall. At the mortuary a doctor found that Ben Hall's body had 15 bullets in it.

Frank Gardiner was jailed, released and ordered out of

Australia. He went, of course, to San Francisco where he became a saloon keeper. In 1903, old Frank was shot during an argument in his saloon over a poker game. In the best outlaw tradition he died with his boots on. Gardiner's sons are said to have searched without success for the gold their father was supposed to have buried near Mount Wheogo, in New South Wales.

Rebellion in the Air
The traffic between the United States and Australia during the gold rush caused a flurry of correspondence between uneasy British diplomats. They worried that subversive ideas of freedom and equality that had infected common men in the United States, were being spread across the Pacific Ocean to start a new epidemic in Australia.

On 30 August 1852, the British Consul in Philadelphia, Williams Peters, sent a confidential despatch to the Foreign Secretary in London, warning him that attempts to establish a republic in Australia were expected. The document was relayed from London to the Governor of Victoria to place him on his guard.

> Hundreds, if not thousands, of adventurers are either now on their voyage, or soon will embark from various parts of the United States for Australia, most of them bent 'on extending the area of freedom' and on aiding their fellow men in the pursuit of Liberty and Republicanism. Indeed an Order, entitled the Order of the Lone Star, had been established here within the last twelve months and for this avowed purpose ... 'to diffuse throughout the world the principles of Liberty and Republicanism ... '
>
> From the knowledge which a residence among them of twelve years has given me of the Americans, and especially of the class of them now on their way to Australia, I do not think that their presence will be attended by much

good, and would have our authorities in that part of the world to be on their guard.

The British Minister in Washington, Crampton, on 31 October 1853, sent yet another confidential despatch to London:

There can be no doubt that a revolution in Australia by which its connections with Great Britain should be severed would be an event highly acceptable to the great mass of the American people.

Australia had rebellious elements, but not sufficiently concentrated for revolution. There was public dislike of authority in all its forms, arising out of authoritarian colonial government. Irish exiles had spread their festering anti-British resentments. Working-class British immigrants in Australia wanted something better than the misery of the British industrial revolution and the social inequalities into which they had been born. Native-born colonials were impatient to be rid of their British governors and to follow the example of the United States into national independence. But endless grumbling substituted for action.

Australia was a country of great distances between home-steads, settlements, and towns. The countryside was sparsely populated. A shifting of population around the colonies during the gold rushes created a sense of impermanence. Revolutionary ideas were difficult to put into practice. The smoke of rebellion was in the air, but not the flames of revolution.

George Train, the American merchant in Melbourne, stated in a letter home that Australia was an embryo republic. He did not give his estimate of the period of gestation.

Train rejoiced over the escape to America of an Irish political prisoner, John Mitchel, who had been on parole in Australia. He took close interest in the colonial electoral system and was angered by its shortcomings. He ridiculed W.C. Wentworth's proposal in Sydney for the establishment of a colonial aristocracy and offered an alternative to all who would listen to him:

'Better a federal government à la America, the centre of which will be Melbourne'. He had been one of the Americans who had given a grand feast in the Criterion Hotel in Melbourne for 150 Irish spreaders of sedition, including that 'patriotic statesman, William Smith O'Brien and his companion in exile, Martin O'Dougherty'. Train declared that the 'cankerous worm of English misrule' had been destroying their unhappy country when the Irishmen 'had thrown themselves into the excitement of the day'.

Train was one of a handful of people at that time who were critical of the inability of the Australian colonies to defend themselves. He pointed out that Australia was an easy mark for any country at war with Britain and that three warships of moderate size could burn every port along the Australian coast. If an armed invasion of Australia occurred, months would elapse before Great Britain could give any assistance.

Train deplored that Australia had no flag of its own. He noted that most of the people in the colony had to pay taxes without being represented in colonial parliaments. Members of the Legislative Council of Victoria were elected for terms of ten years and had to be British-born subjects, aged at least 30, and the owners of freehold property worth at least £10 000. That made the Legislative Council a club for a wealthy few in the 1850s.

American merchants in Melbourne were unhappy about a tonnage duty on all shipping, plus an import tax, but no tax in the colony was more unjust than that imposed by the Colonial Government upon the unfranchised miners of the goldfields. At a time when a labourer could earn only five shillings a day the miners were required to pay a licence fee of 30 shillings a month, payable in advance, and double for Americans. (Governor Hotham reported that of 77 122 men on the goldfields only 43 789 were paying the licence fee – 22 July 1854.)

George Train was of the opinion that the miners were so numerous they could successfully defy the government. He wrote, 'We possess every element of posterity – young in years, but old enough to slip the painter, cut adrift from the old country which hangs over us like an Incubus, and become a nation of ourselves.' It is evident that Train had adopted his new country with a personal and possessive commitment.

American miners on the goldfields were among those involved in daily disputes with police over licences. The Governor, Sir Charles Hotham, arrived in Melbourne in June 1854 to restore the colony's finances and to discipline miners who were not paying the licence tax. Hotham's authoritarian style had been learned during his 36 years in the British Navy and was not suited to the Australia colony he was to govern. Against advice he ordered that all licences be checked at least twice a week. He appointed more police to the goldfields, including former convicts from Tasmania, ex-prison warders, and hoodlums.

One of his police officers was Superintendent Armstrong who became known among the miners as 'the Flying Demon'. Armstrong carried a riding whip with a brass knob on the end of its handle as big as an apple. He used it to club down those who stood in his path. He chained one miner to a tree for two days, although the captive man was ill with bronchitis. The miner died from exposure.

Hotham's law enforcers on the goldfields included informers who kept half of the fines imposed upon miners whom they betrayed to the police. Often the police took a percentage of the informer's cut. Not surprisingly when Superintendent Armstrong was dismissed from his job in disgrace, he left with the defiant comment that he had made £15,000 sterling in two years.

The licence raids continued on the goldfields. Miners were harassed at their work, sometimes being required to climb out of deep mining shafts twice within an hour. Individual miners caught by the police in the open, and without licences, were beaten up. Some were dragged off to prison in their saturated and muddy work-clothes. Tentkeepers, cooks, shopkeepers and the servant of a priest were among those prosecuted for not

owning miners' licences. Outraged miners organised the Ballarat Reform League.

An American named Carey was one of several miners arrested
for rioting. The American Consul, J.M. Tarleton, took a
politely-worded petition to Governor Hotham asking for
Carey's release. Hotham agreed, yielding with prudence to what
was virtually diplomatic intervention on behalf of the United
States Government.

Miners wrote a second petition for the release of the other
men who had been arrested, demanding their release. They
were not at all diplomatic. Hotham was offended by their use of
the word 'demand'. He told the miners:

> The Americans adopted a truly constitutional course in a
> case where they thought themselves aggrieved. They
> signed a petition and presented it in due form through
> their Consul. Have the Ballarat diggers taken the same
> constitutional course? No – I must take my stand on the
> word 'demand'. I'm sorry for it but you leave me no
> alternative . . .

He rejected their request. The non-Americans remained in
custody.

Hotham had decided to appoint a Royal Commission to advise
him on the best methods of raising revenue on the goldfields,
but by then events were moving too fast.

Americans on the goldfields had formed a para-military
organisation. The purpose is now obscure although it could
have had some connection with the American Republican
Order of the Lone Star. Whatever their intentions, it collapsed
with the departure of hundreds who had heard rumours of a
new gold find in South America.

American merchants in Melbourne had been importing
guano from Peru but had not been able to obtain backloading
for their vessels. They had been returning the ships unprofit-
ably across the Pacific in ballast. They solved the problem by

spreading false stories that a new gold bonanza had been discovered in Peru. Between January and March in 1854, twenty-two of the guano ships left Melbourne for Peru carrying miners as backloading, most of them Americans. So awful were conditions in the overcrowded holds of the ships that an estimated 600 died on the voyages before reaching South America and their bodies were thrown into the sea.

A raffish representative of both the Irish and the Americans on the goldfields in Victoria was a man known as 'Captain' Brown. Brown, an Irishman, claimed he had been a Texas Ranger and had lived with the Comanche Indians before travelling to Australia. He also was said to have been a clerk for a slave auctioneer in New Orleans. Soon after his arrival on the Victorian goldfields in 1853, he called a meeting at Bendigo to complain that chaos would result if emigration to Australia continued at the current rate. Before long he switched his attention to a more popular subject, the injustice of high fees for miners' licences.

Following the extremes of the vigilantes in California there was a residual hostility towards Americans at Bendigo, and particularly after an American flag had been raised above a British flag in the presence of British miners. Nevertheless, crowds of men gathered to listen to the Irish/American, 'Captain' Brown, when he made a public speech against high licence fees. Together with a Mr G.E. Thompson and a Dr Jones, Brown formed the Bendigo Anti-Gold Licence Committee, and sent deputies to establish similar bodies at other goldfields.

Brown began using strong-arm tactics to raise money for the committee. A Bendigo storekeeper complained that Brown had threatened to burn him out unless he contributed a substantial sum of money. Brown was arrested by camp authorities. When he tried to threaten them, a magistrate ordered his removal under guard to Melbourne. Exit the Texas Ranger from historical records.

Americans and Eureka
The story of the Eureka Stockade Rebellion is generally well known, but the involvement of Americans has not been mentioned much in history lessons in Australian schools.

On 28 November 1854, Americans at Ballarat gave a dinner to the United States Consul, James Tarleton. Also present were the resident Commissioner to the goldfields, Mr Robert Rede, Police Magistrate, Charles Hackett, and other leading citizens. While the dinner was in progress a messenger arrived hot with news that miners had ambushed a military detachment entering Ballarat.

Commissioner Rede and Magistrate Hackett excused themselves from the dinner and hurriedly left the room. In loud voices the remaining American guests began discussing the latest turn in events. Some wanted to see for themselves what was happening outside but the chairman of the dinner, Mr Otway, and the US Consul, persuaded them to remain where they were and disassociate themselves from the rebellion outside.

Although he was American, Otway proposed a loyal toast: 'Gentlemen, the Queen, God Bless her!'

This was not well received. Sam Irwin, who was Ballarat correspondent of the *Geelong Advertiser*, expressed his feelings: 'While we must demonstrate loyalty to our Sovereign Lady the Queen, God Bless her, we do not and will not, pay our respects to her menservants, her maidservants, her oxen, or her asses.' At that point Irwin indicated the newly vacated chairs of Commissioner Rede and Magistrate Hackett, and others cheered.

In the ambush, a drummer boy had been wounded and several soldiers and the American driver of one of the wagons, George Young of Newburyport, Massachusetts, had been injured. The miners had searched the military convoy for cannon but had not found any.

The following day 12 000 miners assembled at Ballarat and

afterwards flew their flag of independence. It was the Southern Cross, a flag with five white stars on a blue background.

About 1 000 miners, under the leadership of Irishman Peter Lalor, performed an act of treason by swearing allegiance to their new Southern Cross flag. Later it was claimed that Americans had drawn up a Declaration of Independence. A subsequent search for this document was unsuccessful.

The miners began building a defensive stockade upon a low hill facing the military and police camp, using thick slabs of mining timber and saplings and stones. They quickly put up a barrier of doubtful strength enclosing about one acre of land, and prepared to defend it.

One of the Americans who helped build the stockade was a carpenter named Nelson, described afterwards as being a finely built man, full of energy and life. He was put in charge of the best group of defenders but his men came and went as they pleased. They walked home to their tents or went off to work on their distant gold claims when they felt so inclined. As an organised fighting force they were a bad joke.

An Irish-American, James McGill, aged 21, had formed some of his compatriots into the Independent Californian Rangers Revolver Brigade. McGill claimed to have attended a military academy in the United States, but according to some researchers was possibly a lieutenant in US Second Infantry who resigned his commission. George Francis Train afterwards claimed that McGill had hoped to establish a Republic of Victoria, similar to the Lone Star Republic of Texas formed by Sam Houston, or the Bear Flag Republic, which was formed when Americans took California from Mexico only a few years earlier.

Another American, Charles Ferguson from Ohio, who wrote his account of the Eureka Stockade Rebellion, said that a meeting of American miners was held at the Adelphi Theatre in Ballarat to decide what they were going to do. They did not wish to be regarded as cowards. Many of the Americans at the meeting were in favour of enlisting in the 'Digger Army' to fight the troops and police at the diggings. Vainglorious sentiments were expressed.

The rabble of miners within the Eureka Stockade made some attempt to turn themselves into a fighting army. Bellicose Irishmen who did not have any firearms went dashing about with home-made pikes with which they practised thrusts and flourishes. The pikes were long poles with sharpened iron heads manufactured for them by John Hafele, a German blacksmith from Wurtemburg. Peter Lalor commanded at the stockade.

The Independent Californian Rangers Revolver Brigade arrived at the stockade, led by James McGill. An eye-witness, Rafaello Carboni, wrote of McGill, 'You could read in the whites of his eyes, in the colouring of his cheeks, and in the paleness of his lips that his heart is for violence.' Carboni described McGill as being a small but alert man of good presence. He was short and not so much healthy-looking as wide awake. Carboni complained that McGill always seemed anxious to know what was happening – but was not quick to volunteer help.

US Consul Tarleton had been doing his utmost to persuade American citizens on the goldfields to stay clear of the stockade. He was anxious to prevent them from becoming involved in the bloodshed that would surely occur if events continued on their present collision course. The Consul's agent at Ballarat was an American doctor, Charles J. Kenworthy. It has been alleged that Kenworthy arrived at the stockade and urged McGill to withdraw his Californian Rangers.

It was Saturday night, 2 December 1854. The weather for that time of year in Victoria was unusually cold. Many of the miners left the stockade to obtain better shelter at their camps. Other men noted the scarcity of food and water in the stockade and the shortage of guns and ammunition. They intelligently decided not to take part in the coming battle. James McGill placed about one-third of his Rangers around the stockade on guard duty. He then took about 300 of the remaining best-armed men and left the stockade. It was understood that he was going to intercept army reinforcements thought to be on their way to Ballarat from Melbourne. Another account said that he was going to a nearby farming property to bring back a field-gun owned by the landholder.

Military reinforcements under the command of Major General Nickle with guns from two British warships in Melbourne had been ordered to Ballarat, but were not required. Just before dawn on Sunday, 3 December, Commissioner Rede and Captain Wise ordered an attack on the Eureka Stockade. Their force consisted of 152 infantry and 30 cavalry, 74 mounted police and 24 foot police.

The account by Ferguson claims that the first order within the stockade was a shout: 'Californian Rangers to the front!' Ferguson said that one of the Americans, 'Captain' Burnette, took aim with his rifle and fired at the officer in charge of the advancing troops (troops of the Fortieth Foot Regiment), Captain Wise, who fell mortally wounded.

About 22 miners were killed. It is probable that some wounded miners died later in hiding.

The Ballarat correspondent of the *Geelong Advertiser*, Sam Irwin, was an eyewitness. He later described the scene as carts were being sent to collect the casualties.

> They all lay in a small space with their faces upward, looking like lead. Several of them were still breathing and at every rise of their breasts the blood spouted out of their wounds, or just bubbled out and trickled away.

Five of the soldiers had been killed, additional to Captain Wise. Another 12 had been wounded.

The miner, Rafaello Carboni, was arrested while attending to one of the wounded Californians. Carboni had been struck with the deepest admiration for the man and the way he had fought. The Californian had six wounds in his body, all of them in front. Another of the Americans singled out for praise was a black American from New York, named John Josephs. One of the miners' leaders, Joseph Lynche, later wrote of Josephs as 'a coloured gentleman who was arrested in the thick of the fight and who bore himself throughout the ordeal with a great deal of dignity'.

James McGill had become a fugitive, his Californian Rangers Revolver Brigade scattered or captured. The story goes that McGill fled to Melbourne dressed as a woman, passing General Nickle's reinforcements along the way.

The rebel leader, Peter Lalor, was still at large. Like McGill, he had a price on his head. Lalor was recovering slowly from the amputation of his left arm. Rafaello Carboni was in a prison cell, shackled to John Josephs. They were among 14 prisoners charged with treason. The American, Charles Ferguson, was another of the 14 charged.

The Aftermath

While the Crown was preparing for the trials of the prisoners the American Consul, Mr Tarleton, had been working with considerable diplomatic skill to obtain the release of all the Americans who had been captured at the Battle of the Eureka Stockade. Eventually he felt confident enough to send a despatch to the United States Secretary of State in Washington, in which he blandly denied that any Americans had been involved in the uprising.

His was a calculated diplomatic lie. This was exposed by a petition carrying 4 500 names, presented to Governor Hotham in January 1855, and containing this interesting plea:

> If his Excellency had found sufficient extenuation in the conduct of American citizens we thought that there were equally good grounds for extending similar clemency to all, irrespective of nationality; and that it was unbecoming the dignity of any Government to make such exceptions ... We wish it to be distinctly understood by our American friends that we do not for a moment find fault with His Excellency for allowing their countrymen to go

free, but we do claim, in sorrow, that he does not display
the same liberality to others, that he does not wisely and
magnanimously comply with the prayers of our petition
for granting a general amnesty.

The black American, John Josephs, was not an articulate
person, but neither was he simple-minded as he made himself
appear. From the outset of his trial he maintained a disarming
air of bewilderment as his best defence. With the hangman's
noose in mind he played his part well, grinning foolishly and
sometimes whistling before answering questions. Spectators in
the public galleries were convulsed with laughter.

His trial became so ridiculous that Josephs was acquitted. His
sympathisers cheered so loudly that the Chief Judge, Sir William
A'Beckett, obtained the arrest of two of them and sent them to
jail for one week for contempt of court. The second of the
prisoners was acquitted without being required to offer evidence in defence. It was recognised by the court that the jury
intended to acquit all the other defendants too. The Attorney-
General secured an adjournment of the other cases, but one
month later, when they were before the court again, all were
freed.

George Train, (who afterwards returned to the United States
and campaigned for the Presidency as an independent candi-
date), assisted James McGill to escape. He claimed that McGill
turned up at his Melbourne office a few days after the Eureka
Stockade uprising, telling Train he wanted all the Colt revolvers
held in his warehouse. Train said he refused, whereupon McGill
allegedly offered him 'the Presidency of the Republic of
Victoria'. Train would have none of that nonsense. The cause
was lost and Melbourne was back to business as usual. Train
supposedly helped McGill to leave Melbourne, posing as a ship's
officer.

McGill is said to have returned to Ballarat to attend an
anniversary commemoration of the uprising.

Mark Twain wrote about the stockade battle in his book,

Following the Equator – A Journey Around the World. He described Eureka as the finest thing in Australian history and compared it with the conflicts of Concord and Lexington in America – all of them small beginnings but great in political results. Twain visited Australia in 1897.

Within a few years, the Australian gold rush – like the Californian rush that had preceded it – subsided and became part of history. Many of the American miners and merchants who went to Australia during the gold rush remained in the country afterwards, finding new opportunities in an expanding economy. Transportation of British convicts to the Australian colonies had ceased in the middle of the gold rush. (*San Francisco Herald*, 16 June 1852: 'Out of the anti-transportation (of convicts) movement (in Australia) will come a Confederated Republic of the Pacific ... ') Waves of free settlers were providing a new and more expensive source of labour, and were creating a better market for goods and services of all kinds.

Trans-Pacific trade had flourished with the finding of gold. California's population had grown from 93 000 to 380 000 in ten years. Because Australia could supply Californians faster than could the eastern states of America, 86 ships were engaged in the trans-Pacific trade by 1850. Australia exported to California, beer, building materials, flour, timber, and coal. The construction of transcontinental railroads and the opening of the Panama Canal incorporated California into the United States trading zone but diminished the trans-Pacific community of understanding and interest that had developed between California and Australia in the wild frontier days of the gold rushes.

During the decade from 1851 to 1861 the Australian gold rush was mainly responsible for Victoria's population rocketing from 97 000 to 541 000. Melbourne grew from a village of 5 000 to a town of 40 000, larger than San Francisco. (In the ten years after 1851 the non-aboriginal population of Australia almost trebled to 1 200 000. After the gold rush Australia continued to experience an economic boom lasting more than

30 years.)

Legislative reforms after the Eureka Stockade uprising replaced the detested monthly licence tax for goldmining with a miner's right costing £1 a year. This gave holders legal possession of their claims and the right to vote in government elections.

These reforms had been purchased with blood. Some of it was American blood.

3 American Pioneers

Once Australia's new frontiers of European occupation had become more consolidated, closer settlement was required. The original land-grabbers, appropriately called the squatters, had to give up some of their holdings under the Selection Acts. This legislation was based, in part, on America's Homestead Act of 1862.

It could be said that the squatters lived off the land. The selectors, with their smaller holdings, had to work the land. They soon found their lives were not going to be easy. They were helped in their struggle against the harsh Australian environment by farming methods developed by American homesteaders experiencing similar difficulties.

The idea of ringbarking trees reached Australia from the United States. For a century afterwards the Australian country-side was disfigured by the gaunt grey skeletons of forests, still standing where they had been killed decades earlier to allow sunlight to penetrate and grass to grow for sheep and cattle. Ringbarking continued in Australia until after the Second World War when power-saws and bulldozers made land clearance easier – and soil erosion faster.

Other familiar features of the Australian countryside – windmill pumps and barbed wire – also came from America. Stoves and carriages and sewing machines made in the United States were imported and became popular with the Australian public. Lamps in bush shacks at night were burning American kerosene. American ice-boxes helped to preserve food in the hot Australian summers.

In the second half of the nineteenth century American

pioneers who became resident in Australia were responsible for better roads, improved mail services, and for the establishment of many new industries. During the American Civil War they started tobacco-growing and cotton farms in Australia. Irrigation of fruit trees in northern Victoria was based on a system that had been perfected in California and served as a pilot scheme for the great Murrumbidgee irrigation area of later years.

This was a period of progress in Australia when good foundations were being laid for future growth. A less exciting era, perhaps, but a period of development and prosperity.

Mining, Transport and Commerce
One of the most outstanding of all the American pioneers was James Rutherford, who was born in Erie. Rutherford made a fortune in freight and passenger transportation, but was a versatile businessman, successful in all he undertook. He arrived in Australia in 1852, and became a goldminer, a stockman and horse dealer, a stage-coach driver, and then the owner of the Cobb & Co. stage company. He extended coach services from Victoria to New South Wales and Queensland. His company developed the timber trade between Western Australia and India, and constructed the railroad between Glen Innes and Tenterfield in New South Wales. He raised sheep in Queensland, and imported prize bloodstock to improve Australian cattle herds on a scientific breeding basis.

Most important of all, James Rutherford became one of the fathers of the Australian steel industry. He founded and financed the Eskbank ironworks at Lithgow, the forerunner of the BHP iron and steel complex, Australia's most powerful industrial corporation of modern times. Rutherford was that rare combination of adventurer and practical businessman. He died in Queensland in 1911 at the age of 84.

Australia's largest mining and industrial corporation, BHP, was established in August 1885 to mine silver and lead deposits in the south-west of New South Wales. One year later the company recruited expert help in America, engaging William H. Patton as General Manager. Patton had been Superintendent of Consolidated Virginia. He brought in experienced miners from Nevada, adapting American mining methods to the different and often difficult underground problems at Broken Hill in New South Wales.

A metallurgist from Iowa, Herman Schlapp, also was engaged at Broken Hill and supervised the construction of 15 furnaces employing more than 1 000 men. Later, BHP engaged a young consulting engineer in Philadelphia named David Baker who designed for the company a large steelworks at Newcastle, 100 miles north of Sydney. The steelworks was commissioned in 1915. It became the backbone of Australia's heavy industries.

The world's richest gold mine in 1899 was on the Golden Mile at Kalgoorlie in Western Australia and was managed by Henry Clay Callahan from Colorado. Another gold mine nearby, Perseverance, was managed by Ralph Nichols, a mining engineer from New York. A future president of the United States, Herbert C. Hoover, arrived in Australia at the age of 22 and became manager of the Gwalia Mine, 100 miles north of Kalgoorlie.

The story goes that a British Lieutenant-Governor of Western Australia offered young Hoover a tip following a tour of inspection of the mine and its surroundings. The reason is not difficult to understand. Everyone working at Gwalia, including Hoover, its manager, was living in rough conditions in the desert. Their 'homes' were corrugated iron huts. Only the Aborigines had worse shelter.

In 1905, Hoover visited Broken Hill in New South Wales and saw that the tailings from the mining dumps could be treated to extract zinc. He established the Zinc Corporation which became a long-lasting financial success. Hoover was in Australia for two periods, 1896–98 and 1905–07.

A later example of American expertise and dogged determination, backed by money, was the success of the Mount Isa mine in western Queensland. A small company Mount Isa Mines

Limited, had been working during the 1930s to extract lead, silver and zinc from beneath the bare red earth and rocks of the desert. Twice up to 1939 the company had been saved from insolvency by the American Smelting and Refining Company, and had third mortgage debentures underwritten by the Pearl Assurance Company of London.

One of the central figures in the story of persistent work and courage at Mount Isa was an American mining engineer, Julius Kruttschnitt, who had become general manager of Mount Isa Mines Limited late in 1930, and Chairman of Directors in 1937. Kruttschnitt was mainly responsible for keeping the mine going through its poor years, never losing hope that things would improve. His faith was rewarded when massive loads of copper were located.

By 1953 Mount Isa had become the world's richest copper mine and its future was assured. Kruttschnitt retired, stating that the time had come for a younger man to take over his job. Thirteen years later the reserves of copper ore at Mount Isa had been proven up to 41.5 million tons, with grades of up to 3.8 per cent. Since then larger reserves have been located.

The late chief of the Commonwealth Bureau of Mineral Resources in Canberra, Sir Harold Raggatt, had a lasting admiration for Kruttschnitt. In his book, *Mountains of Ore*, published in 1968, Raggatt described him as 'as good an Australian as any native-born Australian I have ever known.'

On the Murray River and its two tributaries, the Darling and Murrumbidgee, small paddle-steamers began carrying wool and other freight from 1853.

They operated between June and December when there was a sufficient flow of water from the 'wet season'. One of the paddle-steamers, the *Lady Daly*, had an American pilot, Captain Peleg Jackson. His American assistant was A.L. Blake. Not surprisingly, the *Lady Daly* flew an American flag.

Another American, Augustus Baker Peirce (known on the river as Captain Gus), from New England, charted 1 360 miles of the Murray River from its mouth to Albury in New South Wales.

He worked from a rowing boat, marking down on tracing paper all the snags and sandbars that he could find in the river. Peirce also placed warning markers on the riverbanks as an additional guide. His charts became invaluable to paddle-boat pilots.

The Murray River paddle-boats needed a lot of wood to fire their boilers. Extensive wood piles became established on the river banks, the wood cutters and their families often living in rough huts in isolated and primitive conditions.

An American named Simmonds established a wood pile near the Wakool Junction that was reputed to be the biggest on the river. It was claimed that if all the wood in the pile was stacked six feet high it would have stretched for one mile along the river bank. Paddle-boat captains travelling along the Murray, Wakool and Murrumbidgee rivers were Simmonds' customers.

His wife, Mary, lived with him near his wood pile. She became pregnant. When her time was almost due she was placed on a paddle-steamer on its way to Swan Hill. The boat had gone only a short distance before Mary Simmonds went into labour. There were complications and both Mary, and the twins she was carrying, died.

Their grave near the river bank at Kenly is a sad reminder of the hardships suffered by some of the pioneers along the Murray River system.

The United States celebrated its centenary in 1876 with a big exposition at Philadelphia in which Australia was an exhibitor of pastoral, agricultural, and mining products. The colony of Victoria exhibited manufactured goods from its industries (protected by high tariffs, including tariff protection against other Australian colonies).

Victorians thought that they would have an exhibition too, in Melbourne. It would celebrate the centenary of the arrival of Captain Arthur Phillip in Australia with the First Fleet and would be the first international exhibition in the Southern Hemisphere. The American brand of enterprise introduced into Victoria in the gold rush had lingered – and the Victorians always welcomed an opportunity to upstage their rivals in the senior Australian colony, New South Wales.

Melbourne's new hall, built for the Centennial Exhibition, was impressive by any international standards. Its dome was claimed to be the biggest and most beautiful in all the world, not excluding the architectural wonders of Washington, London or Rome.

One thousand sailors from visiting foreign warships, including Americans, marched through the streets of Melbourne for the opening of the Centennial Exhibition. American companies occupied 6 000 square feet of space in the exhibition building. Their displays included agricultural machinery, tools and labour-saving devices, printing machines, cash registers and typewriters. The exhibition was widely praised, even in Sydney, where it was recognised as an achievement to be surpassed as quickly as possible.

Melbourne had a modern cable tram system. It had been established by Francis B. Clapp, an American who had been in Australia more than 30 years. The brisk American-style management of Clapp's Omnibus Company rubbed its employees up the wrong way. In 1888 they went on strike. Some of the bus drivers attempted to form a trade union. Clapp sacked them, declaring that he refused to deal with trade unionists on principle. Two hundred men lost their jobs.

Clapp rewarded other employees loyal to the company by giving them an additional week's wage as a bonus. The infant trade union died quietly with Clapp's Yankee grip around its throat.

John Greeley Jenkins was an American politician who did well in Australia. He was born in Pennsylvania in 1851, crossed the Pacific in 1878 as a book salesman and stood successfully for election to the South Australian parliament. He became Premier of South Australia at the turn of the century after having been Minister for Education and Commissioner for Public Works. Jenkins also took government control of the vast and wild Northern Territory.

One of the first big American companies to invest in Australia

John G. Jenkins standing far left (Courtesy SA Archives).

was Mobil Oil Australia which, through the Vacuum Oil Company, had been active in Australia as early as the nineteenth Century. General Electric began trading in Australia in 1898 and manufacturing in Australia in the 1920s. Sterling Pharmaceuticals began operations in Australia in 1910, two years ahead of International Harvester Company of Australia. The Goodyear Tyre & Rubber Company established itself in Australia before the First World War.

After the First World War came the American Foreign Insurance Association, Ford, General Motors, Standard Telephones and Cables, Gilbarker, Kellogg, Kraft, the Wrigley chewing gum company, Colgate Palmolive and many other American companies. Ford established the first automobile industry in Australia with its assembly plant at Geelong in 1925. General Motors accepted the Commonwealth Goverment's invitation to build a complete car for Australia by producing the

Holden in 1948. Ford, Chrysler, and International Harvester, also began developing their versions of an Australian vehicle. As early as 1913, Australia produced 2 000 car bodies. In the same year, it imported another 4 900, mainly from the United States.

Arts and Entertainment
In the arts, Americans who became 'Australians' included the painter, George Washington Lambert (1873–1930); Livingstone Hopkins, from Ohio (1846–1927) was a cartoonist for the Sydney *Bulletin* for more than 30 years; Augustus Earle (1790–1839) published two books of early Australian views, in London; and Joseph Jefferson (1829–1905), an actor, helped to lay the foundations of dramatic art in Australia.

In 1874, J.C. Williamson and his wife arrived from America and presented to Australian audiences a popular melodrama, 'Struck Oil'. They settled in Australia in 1879 and presented Gilbert and Sullivan operas. J.C. Williamson became the best-known theatrical entrepreneur in the country, and his name continued to be seen on billboards in Australia's theatres into the twentieth century. A company formed by J.C. Williamson brought some of the world's best in entertainment to generations of Australians.

Another American, J.D. Williams, rebuilt an old theatre in Swanston Street, Melbourne, in 1911 and ran it as one of the first motion picture houses. He named it the Melba Theatre and ran continuous screenings from 11 a.m. to 11 p.m. The prices were sixpence and threepence, and the seats had real leather cushions. In 1912, Mr Williams built another cinema, the Britannia, next door. It did business until the 1930s. The Melba continued to attract audiences until 1939 when it was rebuilt once more and called the Liberty.

All were American pioneers in Australia in their various fields of knowledge and activity.

In the 1930s, a vaudeville performer from the United States arrived in Sydney and went to work at the Tivoli Theatre. He was Bob Dyer who described himself as the 'Last of the

Hillbillies'. Later he became the king of the quiz shows on Australian radio and television and one of the best-loved entertainers in the country before he retired to Queensland. Dyer also earned fame as a big game fisherman.

A long list of American entertainers followed Dyer to Australia and many of them stayed. Perhaps the money they made was not as much as back home but almost all of them

James C. Williamson.

seemed to make a comfortable living with the approval of Australian audiences filling their pay packets.

Politics

A fire-eating feminist from Texas campaigned for women's rights in Australia. She was Jennie Scott-Griffiths who was born in 1875 in Woodville County. She went to the Pacific islands of Fiji in 1897 where she married the editor of the Fiji Times and had ten children. When the family moved to Australia in 1911, Mrs. Scott-Griffiths ᴸecame the editor of the Australian Women's Weekly in Sydney.

She advocated trade unions for women in employment to help them improve their working conditions and pay, and to obtain for them greater recognition of their skills. Mrs. Scott-Griffiths began contributing to the Women's Page of the *Australian Worker*. She began writing for the *Australian Worker* full-time after being sacked from the Australian Women's Weekly which found her writing style too savage and her political opinions too radical. She took over the editorship of the Women's Page in the *Australian Worker*, following the resignation of Mary Gilmore, a famous Australian writer.

Jennie Scott-Griffiths opposed a move by the Federal Government to conscript reinforcements for the Australian Army fighting in France in the First World War. By then she was also writing for the *Bulletin* and later for the International Socialist.

The Bolshevik Revolution in Russia caught her imagination and sympathies. She became an enthusiastic communist. Conservative government had her placed under surveillance and she was described in security reports as a 'dangerous woman with a vitriolic tongue'. The latter undoubtedly was correct but she fell somewhat short of being a female Lenin of the Southern Hemisphere. It would have been fairer to describe her as an exponent of freedom of speech and ideas and consequently an uncomfortable nuisance to the establishment in Australia.

Jennie Scott-Griffiths moved to Queensland after the First World War and almost immediately was in the midst of new public controversies and political confrontations with police and conservative authority. Only old age subdued her.

By the time of her death in 1951, her numerous progeny were successfully established in business and commercial life in Australia. They were intensely proud of Jennie's colourful career and journalistic exploits, though most of them were wealthy conservatives who abhorred communism.

The first Federal Parliament met in Melbourne in May 1901. An American journalist, Jessie Ackermann, who spent several years in Australia at the beginning of the twentieth century, complained that all its members were men. Even when the same parliament gave women the right to vote in federal elections in 1902, she did not relent.

Jessie Ackermann wrote:

> Every once in a while some member (of Parliament) rises, halo in hand, to anoint himself high priest and claim the glory touch of shepherding the women into the kingdom of federal citizenship . . .

She suggested that the true reason why Federal Parliament had enfranchised women was to make them sympathetic to certain members of the Parliament and catch their votes. She continued:

> In different States, the possibility of making Party use of women's votes has been regarded as legitimate reason for granting female suffrage . . .

Jessie was cynical and difficult to please, but she knew her politicians.

Although the authors of the Australian Constitution used the Constitution of the United States at the end of the nineteenth century as a reference in their deliberations, there was much bickering and rivalry over a period of ten years between inter-colonial leaders, and much compromising. They decided that

Australia would remain a dominion of the Mother Country within the British Empire and that her citizens would continue to be subjects of the British sovereign.

Formal recognition of the constitutional independence of the central Australian government from Britain was not effected until 1942 when the Statute of Westminster was adopted. Australia's constitutional independence was then made retrospective to the country's entry into the Second World War in September 1939, but the Constitutions of each of the States of Australia remained subordinate to the British Parliament legally, right up to the time this book was being written. It was a bizarre situation, a left-over from the time when each State was a separate British colony.

The Australian Federal Constitution blended traditional features of British-style government with elements adopted, or adapted, from the Constitution of the United States. For instance, the allocation of powers between federal and state governments was on the American pattern. The central government had responsibility for postal services, customs and excise, defence and foreign relations. The six state governments within the Australian federation remained autonomous in all matters not specifically delegated to the federal government.

In the first half of the nineteenth century, Governor Darling in Sydney and Governor Arthur in Hobart had sent newspaper editors to prison for trying to influence public opinion in favour of democracy and self-rule. Earlier colonial governors had silenced some of their more out-spoken critics by having them flogged. Governor Darling once described his legal officer, Chief Justice Forbes, as a republican who held 'Yankee principles'. Justice Forbes had been resisting attempts by the British to toughen colonial administration.

The Commonwealth Constitution of Australia did not specifically protect the freedom of the press. American law provided that public figures could not succeed in suits for libel unless they could show that the wounding words were a deliberate lie or that the reporter was recklessly indifferent to their truth or falsehood. Damages for libel were much easier to obtain in Australia than in the United States.

The Federal Attorney General, Herbert Vere Evatt, on 15 March 1944 introduced an amendment to the Australian Constitution. Evatt, a former Justice of the High Court of Australia, proposed 'Neither the Commonwealth nor a State may make any law for abridging the freedom of speech or of expression'. Evatt said he believed that the function of speech was to free men from irrational fears. He quoted Justice Lewis Brandeis of the US Supreme Court who had said that the remedy to falsehood in public debate was 'more speech, not enforced silence'.

Evatt's amendment won majorities in the States of Western Australia and South Australia but was lost because it was lumped in with a package of proposals to temporarily expand federal powers. The Australian public was too resentful of over-government to grant more powers to politicians. It was willing to jettison greater freedom of speech to block the other federal proposals.

O'Malley and Griffin

An American was one of the members of the first Australian Federal Parliament. He was King O'Malley, a flamboyant man who started his working life in his uncle's bank in the United States and later was in sawmilling and real estate in Wichita, Kansas. In 1880 at the age of thirty, O'Malley emigrated to Australia. He was interested in politics and stood for the State House of Assembly for the seat of Encounter Bay in South Australia. O'Malley claimed conveniently when standing for public office that he had been born in Canada, a part of the British Empire. He never disclosed exactly where in Canada this occurred and it remains doubtful.

O'Malley made three promises during his election campaign. He undertook that if he got into parliament he would legislate so that children born out of wedlock would become legitimate once their parents married. He promised that he would prevent women from working as barmaids in local pubs because they were a temptation to all decent family men. O'Malley further pledged that he would strive his utmost to have lavatories provided on passenger trains in South Australia.

O'Malley had found the recipe for electoral success that many Australian politicans have followed since. Political promises become electorally attractive when they deal with basic social issues that can be readily understood by the public. Such promises should be delivered with humor and rhetoric to make them sound entertaining as well as professional and should not cost the taxpayers much money.

O'Malley did not fail the people of Encounter Bay. Through his efforts all three of his promised reforms became law in South Australia.

In 1911, when King O'Malley was Minister for Home Affairs, his ambition to establish a federal capital city for Australia, similar to Washington, was realised. The Government selected as the site an attractive plain midway between Sydney and Melbourne, inhabited mainly by sheep and cattle. It was on the fringe of the Australian Alps with an altitude of 2 000 feet. It had the strategic advantage of being more than 100 miles inland, and therefore out of range of the guns of foreign warships. This had strong appeal to politicians and public servants who would have to live there. (O'Malley suggested that the new Australian federal capital be called Shakespeare).

The Australian Government received good advice from architects of the district of Columbia in the United States, based upon experience gained from the failure of the original scheme for the construction of the city of Washington. A French engineer, Major Pierre Charles L'Enfant, who had designed the American capital, had worked under the close supervision of George Washington and Thomas Jefferson, but too many of his proposals had been rejected or overruled. As a result, modern Washington was a travesty of what had been planned. It bore little resemblance to L'Enfant's original blueprints, having overgrown the countryside far beyond the first orderly limits for the city. In 1901, the United States Senate had appointed a committee to consider what steps could be taken to restore the city of Washington to its earlier concept. After a full investigation, the committee found that it was too late and too costly to rescue Washington from indiscriminate developments. So it continued.

Australians were warned to heed the mistakes made in Washington when they built their own new capital.

An international competition was launched by King O'Malley for a design for Canberra. Apart from having been a real estate salesman, King O'Malley lacked any qualifications to be the adjudicator of the competition. When it was publicly announced that he intended to be the adjudicator, the Royal Institute of British Architects, the Institute of Civil Engineers, and affiliated bodies within the British Empire nations, boycotted the competition in protest. O'Malley and the Australian Government refused to back down. O'Malley remained the adjudicator, although with the assistance of an expert committee of advisers.

A total of 137 designs was submitted, some ridiculous, some magnificent. By a majority decision the committee of advisers decided that Mr Walter Burley Griffin, of Chicago, had provided the best design. The adjudicator declared Griffin the winner. The fact that he was a fellow-American had nothing to do with it.

Although only 34 years of age, Griffin had an international reputation. He had planned the reconstruction of Shanghai. He also had been a partner of the up-and-coming young genius, Frank Lloyd Wright, of Chicago. Most of his associates had been predicting that Griffin's future career would be more illustrious than that of Wright, who had an erratic character. Indeed, when Griffin won the Australian competition to design Canberra, his former partner was somewhere in Europe, hiding from his creditors.

Walter Burley Griffin was a shy and artistic man but his backbone was stiffened by professional pride. The opportunity to design a federal capital city in the pastoral hinterland of

Australia had for him great romantic appeal. He saw it as a chance to earn for himself a place in architectural history.

Griffin was fortunate in having as his assistant a brilliant draftswoman, Marion Mahoney, who had been one of the first women to become an architect in the State of Illinois. She helped him with his design for Canberra. After it won the competition they married.

At the Univeristy of Illinois, Griffin had learned of the mistakes made in the planning of Washington. He tried to avoid them in his Canberra design. He drew up a plan which radiated outwards in a series of expanding circles from a central hill through a carefully planned road network, forming the skeleton of the future city. Griffin hoped that this would ensure that Canberra kept its integrity of design as it grew. In his plan he provided for a generous allocation of parklands and for a series of small shopping centres, all within easy walking distance of each dormitory neighbourhood, as were also the schools. Canberra would be a spacious city, but comfortable, with all community amenities easily accessible. Griffin hoped to save the federal capital of Australia the traffic confusion and slums of most major cities in the United States.

He planned Canberra to be a city in which strict zoning would prevent factories and repair shops from intruding into residential areas, and which also would prevent overcrowding and overdevelopment in any one sector. As the city grew, the zoning plan could be repeated in other areas held in reserve by the Government. Thus the size of every self-contained district of the city would be regulated; the balance between residential, industrial, and shopping, and service amenities would be maintained.

In the rustic Australia of that era, not everyone admired the splendour of Griffin's planning. Some said that his winning design for Canberra was too elaborate. Others reached with a knife for the Government's hamstring, alleging that the plan required extravagant expenditure of government funds.

Foundation stones for Canberra were laid by the Governor-

General, Lord Denman, the Prime Minister, Andrew Fisher, and by the Minister for Home Affairs, King O'Malley, in that order of priority. Considering Australia's history, it was significant that an American joined the British Governor-General and the Australian Prime Minister in the ceremony.

Holding a trowel made from Australian gold, and with which he ceremoniously tapped the foundation stone, O'Malley engaged in oratory. He declared:

> Our own evolutionary peaceable revolution that might have been productive of a 30 years war has been accomplished. Six independent States and territories are federated with one national government overall, so just and free that many wonder its achievement should have been so successful.

He added that God had commanded the English-speaking peoples to secure the control of and constitutionally govern the Earth in the interests of civilisation.

O'Malley's speech impressed the former colonials who had assembled for the occasion. It made them feel that at last their country had come of age. The spectacle of Lord Denman standing there in his splendid British uniform reassured them that although they had become 'independent' in an isolated continent on the edge of Asia, and 12 000 miles from the Mother Country, Britain had not forgotten them, and would continue to protect them from all harm.

That made nationhood less frightening.

In August 1913, Walter Burley Griffin arrived in Australia, eager to begin work. He had been appointed Federal Capital director of Design and Construction in Canberra for a term of three years and with the right to have his own private practice. Some Australian officials, however, saw him as a Yankee outsider who intruded into their domain of authority. History began to repeat itself. Griffin and the plan for Canberra began to undergo the same misfortunes that had befallen L'Enfant and the city plan for Washington. Griffin's Australian opponents set out to do everything within their powers to entangle him in red tape and to sabotage his endeavours.

Griffin was tempted to abandon Canberra and return to a more intellectually responsive, sophisticated and discerning society in Chicago where he could have ridiculed 'hillbilly' Australian officialdom. But instead of surrendering and returning home, as his wife urged him to do, Griffin stayed on to fight every move made against him.

The reluctance of the United States to enter World War I aroused wide-spread anti-American feeling within the Australian nation. Griffin, an American in Australia, had to take some of the brunt of it. In Parliament one day, a former Minister for Home Affairs, Mr Archibald, referred to Griffin as being 'a Yankee bounder'-- an insulting British expression of that time. Archibald added that in his opinion the American system of doing business was to try to undermine others. Archibald was an authority on that subject.

A Royal Commission was appointed to investigate allegations that there had been a conspiracy between Archibald and senior government officers to prevent Griffin from carrying out his duties in building Canberra. Witnesses established conclusively that buidings and municipal services had been constructed in Canberra without Griffin's approval and contrary to the city plan. Griffin's advice had been ignored. Contour maps of the city's environs had been supplied to him by the Department of Home Affairs in the wrong scale. On one map, supplied by the Government to Griffin, someone had wrongly marked a depression in the ground as a hill.

The Royal Commissioner found that Griffin had been hampered wilfully and seriously in his duties, that necessary information and assistance had been withheld from him, and that his powers had been usurped by certain government officers. The Commissioner found that a hostile combination working against Griffin had included the former Minister for Home Affairs, Archibald the Underminer, though not quite in those words.

A new Prime Minister, William Morris Hughes, ended the connection of both Griffin and O'Malley with Canberra. O'Malley fell out first with Hughes over the national issue of whether or not Australian men would be conscripted for the battlefields of France. Until then, all Australian soldiers in the war had been volunteers, but casualties had become so heavy that the Australian Army was in danger of being shot out of existence unless reinforced with conscripts. Prime Minister Hughes, an immigrant from Britain, was in favour of conscription. O'Malley, an immigrant from the United States, opposed it. So too did the Australian public. A referendum was held, and Hughes' conscription proposal was defeated.

Hughes left the Labor Party to form a new policital machine. He kept control of the Government, pushing O'Malley and others of his former colleagues into Opposition. O'Malley struggled on but was defeated in the general elections of 1917 and again in 1919. The wider spread of anti-Americanism grown out of the war probably contributed to O'Malley's loss of popular support. It was widely believed in Australia that the United States had delayed its entry into the war for business profits, and that money meant more to Americans than honour. National emotions were running high. Australia had sent 325 000 volunteers overseas to the war and of these 213 000 had become battle casualties – and this out of a total population of less than four and half million!

Walter Burley Griffin remained in Canberra after the political eclipse of King O'Malley, but came into increasing conflict with Prime Minister Hughes. He steadfastly refused to obey instructions that he must accept compromises and change his city design. One day in 1920 the Prime Minister sent him a brusquely worded note, ending his contract after the expiry of the current term. Griffin was sacked.

Fortunately, the further development of Canberra was delayed by diminished public funds between the two world wars. Some unplanned temporary buildings and sheds were erected after Griffin's departure by people who seemed determined to turn Canberra into an Australian bush town. But not much harm was done. Meddling bureaucrats who would have ruined Griffin's design had they been given sufficient money to spend were kept short. The reluctance of politicians and government officials to move to Canberra from their homes in Sydney or Melbourne also slowed down development.

A building boom began in Canberra after the Second World War. By then a new generation of enlightened administrators recognised the true value of the American designer's work. His plans for the city were staunchly defended. Canberra became one of the few cities of the modern world to be planned from its earliest beginnings; free from poor districts; a city of government, public administration and dignity; but also a comfortable city in which to live. Its tourist industry thrived on tax-payers who came visiting to see where their money had gone.

After leaving politics, King O'Malley formed a business syndicate which purchased one square mile of land on the north side of Sydney Harbour from Lord Carrington for 15 000 pounds sterling. Later the same area of real estate was to soar in value to somewhere around $1 billion. The Carrington family must still wince when they remember that sale to the former American real estate man, O'Malley, in 1921.

O'Malley wanted to give Griffin an opportunity to show what he could do with designs for suburban development. His syndicate formed the Greater Sydney Development Company with Griffin as managing director. The company developed the one square mile as a distinctive new suburb called Castlecrag.

Griffin offered five miles of waterfront of Sydney Harbour to the municipal authorities as a park. Incredibly, his offer was declined. The invaluable five miles of waterfront, offered to the aldermen as a gift, was sold instead to private buyers. The land became built-out to the waterline, excluding a few narrow routes of public access.

The homes that Griffin designed at Castlecrag, and others in Melbourne, were among the first in Australia to satisfactorily meet local conditions. They established a standard for modern

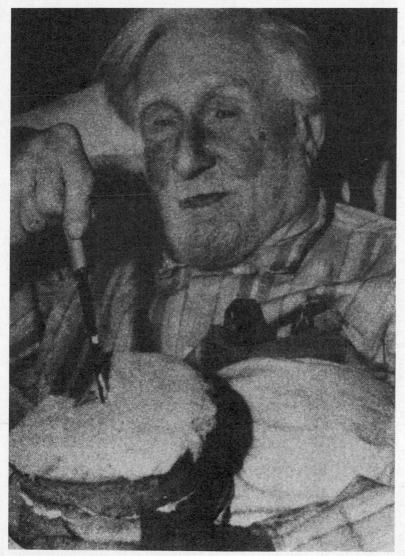

King O'Malley celebrating his birthday shortly before he died.

domestic architecture. One of Griffin's inventions was the use of lightweight concrete building blocks which revolutionised the Australian building industry.

In 1928, Griffin told a meeting of the Theosophical Society in Sydney that the chief curse on the practice of architecture and engineering in Australia was an overbalanced power of government. It had placed the shackles of mediocrity on individual freedom and scope of opportunity.

In 1935, Griffin won a competition to design a new library for the University of Lucknow in India. His arrival there was hailed with excitement. Soon he was building palaces for rajahs, and had become a friend of Mahatma Ghandi. Twelve months later his life came to an end. He fell from scaffolding on a building site, ruptured his gall bladder, and died from peritonitis.

King O'Malley survived to strut the shining avenues of Canberra. In the Commonwealth Bank, which he had helped to establish, were ample funds for his needs; and in his wallet was always a comfortable wad of the paper currency he had helped to introduce. At the age of 90, O'Malley gave his occupation in a census return as that of 'Bishop of Water Lily Rock Bound Church, the Redskin Temple of the Chickasaw Nation'. He amused himself occasionally by exchanging insults in letters to the editors of newspapers with another ancient of Australian politics, William Morris Hughes, the former Prime Minister. Sometimes, while making a radio broadcast, O'Malley would recall his past exploits. From radios all over Australia would issue his cackling laughter. In December 1953, O'Malley died at the age of 95, leaving most of his fortune to charity. His indignant old widow went to court to claim an increase in the allowance which he had allotted to her. But O'Malley's judgement had been sound. His widow died soon afterwards with most of her allowance unspent.

4   Defence, Trade, Wars

Australia's Early Defence

Australians hoped that distance and the logistic problems of fuel and supply would defeat the enemies before they reached their far-away country. The British Navy could finish off any who did manage to get through. Britannia ruled the waves as everyone knew. But in 1879, a British Royal Commission found that most empire defences were weak. Long before that many Australians were scared.

An American ship carrying a naval scientific expedition commanded by Charles Wilkes dropped anchor in Sydney Harbour after dark on 29 November 1839. No one in Sydney knew about it until morning. An invasion force could have taken Sydney overnight while its citizens were sleeping. This caused such alarm that the authorities fortified a rocky island in the harbour and called it Fort Denison. During the next century one of its cannons were fired at noon every day to tell Sydney people the time and keep them on their toes.

Thirty years after the American entrepreneur George Francis Train observed that a few enemy warships could lay waste most of Australia's coastal settlements without much opposition, the country's defences had not improved. In 1882, residents of the seaside town of Glenelg, only six miles from Adelaide, came out one morning, yawning and rubbing their eyes, and found a Russian fleet anchored comfortably off-shore. The Russians were friendly. They accepted local entertainment and invitations to a Grand Ball. The Governor of South Australia also went to the ball wearing an appropriate vice-regal expression.

As soon as the Russian fleet departed, the colonists of South

Australia began strengthening their defences. They built a strategic railway and a military road. They imported two large guns from England, mounting them in the sandhills overlooking the coast. These quickly became stained with seagull droppings. Decades passed peacefully and the guns corroded in the salt air. Picknickers stuffed their lunch wrappings down the muzzles rather than be untidy.

Despite such practical defence preparations, another body of opinion in Australia thought the colonies should hedge their bets by encouraging the United States of America to protect them. In 1908, one of the country's first Prime Ministers, Alfred Deakin, asked the American Government to send a battle fleet on a visit. He hoped this would establish a useful precedent.

Relations with Britain

Apart from occasional nationalistic outbursts, the Australian colonies remained loyal components of the British Empire, and had been paying their membership dues. In 1900, an Australian contingent had joined Britain, Germany, Japan and the United States in an international expedition to China to enforce the American policy that China must accept trade with the western world (and exploitation). In 1885 colonists from New South Wales had gone to help empire forces at Sudan.

The colony of Victoria and Canada quickly offered to send forces too but Britain turned them down. In the Victorian Legislative Assembly, Gyles Turner said that it was a prostitution of terms to claim patriotic virtue for the New South Wales men 'who were ready to shoot Arabs, negroes, Abyssinians or Egyptians indifferently at five shillings a day'.

Sixteen thousand Australian volunteers served with the British Army in the Boer War between 1899 and 1902 to put down the rebellion of fellow-colonists, amid an upsurge of loyalty for the 'Mother Country'. As this happened at the beginning of Australian Federation, it ended 'treasonable' ideas for establishment of an Australian republic. The First World War similarly recharged Australian loyalties to Britain, though at the same time reinforcing nationalism. British governments remained insensitive to Australia's uneasiness about its close proximity to Asia. In particular, Australians became indignant about Britain's military alliance with Japan, and its assistance in Japan's modernisation of its armed forces, especially the Japanese Navy.

Australians in a general sense did not like or trust Asians. There had been riots against Chinese goldminers in Australia, beginning at Lambing Flat, in New South Wales, in 1860-61. An estimated 40 000 Chinese miners were in Victoria in 1859 and 10 000 in NSW in 1861. Chinese miners had been used as strike-breakers in Victoria in 1873 and were hated for it. Public hostility towards Asian immigrants in Australia continued and in 1902 a Restrictive Immigration Act was introduced and the White Australia Policy began. The British Government, however, successfully put pressure on Australia to exclude Japanese businessmen and their families from its immigration restrictions.

With British encouragement and training, the Japanese rapidly increased their naval power, and defeated a Russian fleet in the war of 1904–05 – the first Asian victory over a modern western power. Australian newspapers made the accurate prophecy that the Japanese Navy could one day turn its might against Australia. Britain had been helping to create a menace, a belligerent and now triumphant Japan avid for an empire of its own.

America and Australia
That was the background to the tumultuous public welcome given to the American fleet when it visited Australia in August and September 1908 in response to Prime Minister Deakin's invitation. One hundred thousand people gathered at vantage points around Sydney Harbour to witness the arrival of 16 battleships under the command of Rear Admiral Charles S Sperry. Sydney had been lavishly decorated in preparation for the occasion. A replica of the Statue of Liberty five stories high

A souvenir of the 1908 visit of the Great White Fleet (Courtesy Mitchell Library).

had been built in front of the *Daily Telegraph* offices. A *Telegraph* reporter wrote:

> The Great White Ships. . . a long strong hard-hitting arm, ready to strike terrible blows in defence of the white man's cause should it ever be assailed in this part of the world. . .

He was a racist and proud of it. But he was a nervous racist.

Admiral Sperry cautiously acknowledged compliments without committing his country to Australia's defence in any future conflict with Japan or anyone else. America was unaligned and isolationist in her foreign policies and would not be seduced into any premature ANZUS treaty by flag-waving Aussies.

The flagship of the fleet was *USS Connecticut* of 16 000 tons, and five other battleships in the fleet were of equal size. All the American vessels were among the best of the world's fighting ships. They were exactly what Australians wished to see off their defenceless coastline – as long as they were American and friendly.

The *New York Times*, *Herald*, *Tribune* and other newspapers in America ran stories expressing astonishment over the reception given to the fleet in Australia. A correspondent of the *New York Herald* wrote that 'The Australian friendship will not be forgotten. . . Australians are truly kinsmen, and the word will stick'. A correspondent for the *New York Sun* commented jocularly, 'The only possibility is for us to admit them (Australia and New Zealand) as states within our Federal Union'.

American pressmen covering the south-west Pacific cruise of the Great White Fleet, reported to their newspapers that Britain must be feeling mighty uncomfortable about Australian suggestions that the United States should proclaim a New Monroe Doctrine for the defence of the Pacific.

The United States Navy was not so pleased when more than 300 of its sailors deserted. Over 200 of them, assisted by Australian girlfriends and hidden in Australian homes, were never picked up. Including the men who had deserted earlier in New Zealand, the fleet lost the equivalent of an entire crew of one of its battleships, most of them casualties fallen to Cupid's arrows.

Naval chiefs in London were indeed worried by the resounding success in American public relations achieved by the visit. They did not miss the inference that Australians saw themselves as citizens of outposts of empire, vulnerable but neglected by London. An imperial conference was held and a new system of British naval defence for her Pacific dominions eventuated. It included the creation of a Pacific fleet in three divisions, each led by a battle-cruiser and based respectively in China, the East Indies and Australia. The China and East Indies divisions would remain under British control, but the Australian sector would be financed, controlled and manned entirely by Australians.

Ten years later the price for Britain's policy commitment to the defence of Australia was paid. Australian losses in the First World War were the highest casualty rate of an empire army.

In September 1918, in one of the last battles of the First World War, two American divisions came under the command of the Australian general, John Monash. Fighting together as a co-ordinated army, the Australians and the Americans broke through the German resistance on the Hindenberg Line. (The Australian Official War History notes that American troops competed against the Australians in the advance in a spirit of rivalry).

The discomforts of sea travel in this period, before airline passenger services became commonplace, resulted in at least one American becoming an involuntary resident of Australia – and probably there were others. Jack Teague of Kansas City travelled to New Zealand on holidays where he met and married a local girl. He was taking Patti, his bride, back to the United States but she became so seasick crossing the Tasman that when the couple arrived in Sydney, she refused to go any further. Nor would she return to New Zealand. Once across the Tasman was enough for her.

The Teagues settled in Sydney for the remainder of their lives. Jack Teague found employment with Sydney's tramway system. He was popularly known as 'Jack the Yank', well-liked and respected. The Teagues lived at Paddington in Sydney and became friends of the parents of the author of this book.

The 1930s Depression
A trade war made life uncomfortable for Americans living in Australia in the 1930s. Relations between the governments of Australia and the United States cooled. The trouble arose out of the Depression.

Economist Angus Maddison wrote in his *Phases of Capitalistic Development* that in 1870 Australia had the highest per capita income in the world, 173 per cent above that of the United States. At the turn of the century, Australia was still a working man's paradise. Housing standards were high and people had more to spend than workers elsewhere in the world. Food was cheaper in relation to income than anywhere else, except some sections of North America. Meat consumption was two or three times Britain's and four times Germany's. By the outbreak of the First World War, Australia still had the highest per capita GDP in the world, but other nations were rapidly closing the gap. By the Great Depression of 1929, the United States, Switzerland and Belgium were doing better than Australia. (Unemployment in Australia reached more than 35 per cent and thousands of the jobless roamed the countryside.)

Australia's overseas borrowings almost ceased because of the slump in Britain. World export markets, and prices, for Australia's farm products diminished. Soon the country was in financial difficulties. It was unable to increase its earlier borrowings or pay the interest on outstanding debts. It became short of money to import essential goods.

In a futile attempt to get out of trouble, Australia increased her wheat exports by 80 per cent in volume, doubled her butter exports, increased beef exports by a third, flour by a quarter, and wool exports by almost 10 per cent.

At a time when many people in the world were starving and dressed in rags, Australia had for sale a huge abundance of food and fibre but could not earn sufficient money to import other necessary requirements. Her greatly increased exports of commodities were down in value to only 55 per cent of the total sales return on the same range of products, but in much lower volume, exported before the Depression.

Britain and the empire had failed as a secure market for Australian exports. In desperation, Australia turned towards the United States. America was buying from Australia only one-sixth as much as it was selling in return. Pleas failed, so the Australian Government decided to take stern action. It introduced discriminatory duties, quotas and import licensing against American products in an attempt to force increased US purchasing of Australian goods. It took similar action against Japan.

The United States Government retaliated. For two years, almost to the start of the Second World War, Australia was one of only two nations in the world not receiving 'most favoured nation' treatment in trade with the United States. The other country sharing this American displeasure was Nazi Germany.

The Second World War
As Germany and Japan prepared for war, the chronic unpreparedness of Australians to defend their great continent against attack was even worse than usual. But when Britain was compelled by the invasion of Poland in September 1939 to declare war on Germany, the Prime Minister of Australia, Robert Menzies, hurriedly followed suit, once more paying his country's dues for empire membership and the collective security that this was supposed to secure.

Apart from the fact that Australia had little strength to fight anyone, the phraseology used by Prime Minister Menzies humbled any of his countrymen who had imagined they belonged to an independent nation. Menzies broadcast over radio: 'Great Britain has declared war and as a result Australia is also at war'. Evidently there had been no choice in the matter. When Britain played a tune Australia still had to dance to it. Perhaps Menzies intended his words to be an unqualified demonstration of 'family loyalty', of empire unity; but they also implied Australia's subordinate status as a dominion of Britain – 39 years after King O'Malley had boasted of the nation's independence on Federation Day (Constitutionally Menzies probably was correct as the Commonwealth of Australia did not adopt the Statute of Wesminster until 1942).

The Second World War was to tear the British Empire apart, end Australia's historic reliance upon British protection, and create a new alliance with the United States. It would bring a fresh influx of Americans into Australia.

The American Involvement
On Glebe Island in Sydney is a plaque to commemorate the landing there of one million US servicemen in the Second World War and 20 million tons of US war materials.

The men and women of the American armed forces who were in Australia during three of the war years made a profound

impact on the country. It could be said that they americanised
the capital cities in which they spent their money and temporarily transferred to the United States the regional areas of
Australia where they trained. Their influence on Australian
attitudes was powerful and caused many changes.

When they arrived they found what they saw as a country that
was still in many ways a colonial backwater, self-satisfied and
easy-going, although suddenly anxious under the threat of a
Japanese invasion. With the brash frankness said to be charac-
teristic of their race, Americans newly-landed proclaimed that
Australia was out of date. It was where the United States had
been 20 or 30 years ago. With more tact, others said that
Australia reminded them of the conservative mid-west states of
America. They were also out of date.

The American armed forces imported Yankee hustle into
Australia. To meet the emergencies of wartime they got things
done in a hurry. This was in sharp contrast to the leisurely
manner in which many Australians still worked. An apocryphal
story often told in early 1942 alleged that an American
commander was so impatient to take possession of newly-arrived
war supplies on a dock in Sydney that he used an army tank to
smash down the traffic gates when he found them chained and
padlocked and the man with the only set of keys away for lunch.

The money spent in Australia by US service personnel and by
the US Government enriched commerce and industries. The
American way of life, imported and preserved intact among the
US armed forces in Australia during the war, was a cultural
shock. The Australian public was fascinated by the Americans'
manner of speech, their customs and behaviour. In total, it was
the sudden impact of the people of a much more competitive,
sophisticated, richer and more populous country upon those of a
smaller and relatively backward one.

The same thing happened elsewhere in the world to an even
greater degree during the war but the lesson to Australians was
chastening. Most of them had never before been in close
comparative contact with a foreign people. So distant was

Australia from the rest of the world that until the Second World War pedestrians in city streets would turn and stare in surprise if they heard a foreign language being spoken. Until the Americans arrived with their advanced equipment in great abundance and variety, many Australians had a rather inflated opinion of their own country's place in the world. The American occupation force with its confident and superior attitude, fine uniforms and fat rolls of dollar bills, brought Australians back to reality with a bang. Young Americans in Australia in their hundreds of thousands upset the established order of things.

But they were needed.

The Pacific Struggle
In October 1941, when the Labor leader, John Curtin, became Prime Minister, he found that industry was working at only 50 per cent of its capacity. Almost all Australia's trained fighting men were overseas helping to defend Britain's empire. (They were helping to guard the Suez Canal and Singapore was part of Australia's 'forward defence' strategy in 1939.) The outgoing government, led by Prime Minister Menzies, had left only 5 000 men of the permanent military forces at home. (Additional to being Prime Minister, Menzies was Minister for Co-ordination of Defence, 1939–41.) The so-called Home Army was virtually non-operational. Its few anti-tank guns had only 15 rounds of ammunition per gun. Its few field artillery guns of First World War vintage had less than one week's supply of ammunition. Its hastily recruited civilian soldiers had only 6 per cent of their total requirements of rifles and only 20 per cent of their required number of submachine guns.

Prime Minister Curtin was told that not one modern fighter plane was available in Australia. On the beaches around Sydney, older men of the Volunteer Defence Corps were going on patrols with cadet rifles for which there was no ammunition at all. In the 'Home Army' youthful recruits began drilling with broomsticks.

On 27 December 1941, Prime Minister Curtin, Menzies'

Wife of the US President, F. D. Roosevelt, Eleanor, arrives in Rockhampton at the start of her Queensland tour, 9 September, 1943. Mrs Roosevelt came to Australia to meet members of the American forces in camps, hostels and hospitals. She is wearing the uniform of the American Red Cross worker (Courtesy John Oxley Library).

replacement, made it known that Australia looked to the United States as its only hope. In his appeal to America, he said:

> The Australian Government regards the Pacific struggle as primarily one in which the United States and Australia must have the fullest say in the direction of the democracies' fighting plan. Without any inhibitions of any kind I make it clear that Australia looks to America, free of any pangs as to our traditional links of kinship with the United Kingdom.

Five days earlier, on 22 December, the first US troops and some artillery had arrived in four ships, including the heavy cruiser, *Pensacola*. Other American help soon followed. In northern Australia, air-fields were laid down by Americans for US fighter squadrons. American reinforcements orginally intended for the Philippines were diverted to Australia not a moment too soon. The public welcomed the Americans with a huge but premature sense of deliverance.

The war reached the Australian mainland with the bombing of Darwin on 19 February 1942. Americans were among the first killed. The Japanese sank eight ships, destroyed 23 aircraft, killed 243 people and wounded 320 others, many of them civilians. One of the ships sunk in Darwin Harbour was the American destroyer, *Peary*, which went down with its guns still firing. As the destroyer rolled over on its side, those of its crew still alive had to jump into a harbour ablaze with oil.

February 1942 was a month of horror for the United States and Australia. The US forces besieged in the Philippines were in the final throes of being battered into submission. An Australian army, sent to Malaya as part of the empire defence concept, was captured almost to a man in the British base of Singapore where the fortress guns were fixtures, pointing out to sea and away from the Japanese land approach.

The British and American war strategists saw global defence gaps everywhere and all seemed to them to have greater significance than the defence of the Australian continent. Britain's war chiefs side-tracked returning Australian units of the Overseas Army to garrison Ceylon at the foot of India where nothing happened. They stopped other good Australian troops from getting home to defend their country by landing them in Java where they were wasted almost immediately against an overwhelming force of Japanese invaders. All were killed or captured.

Australian troops brought home from the Middle East showed their disdain for the untried Americans they found training in their country. The Australian expeditionary troops had fought with distinction against Rommel's Africa Korps at Tobruk and at El Alamein. They had fought the French Foreign Legion and had captured Italians by the thousands. In Greece they had been in battle with Germany's stormtroopers and in Crete they had opposed German paratroops. They found MacArthur's men unimpressive from the officers down. This was noted by US Lieutenant General Robert L. Eichelberger, who reported:

> Although Australian officers are too polite to say it to us they think that the U.S. soldiers are insufficiently trained and inexperienced theorists.

Conflict on the Home Front

During the wartime occupation of Australia by the armed forces of the United States, families received the Americans into their homes. They arranged vacations for them in the countryside. Women ran canteen services for them in the cities. Lasting friendships were made.

Few Australian women were accustomed to flattery or to the compliments and attentions American women took for granted, or demanded and received as their right. They reacted favourably to American courtesies. Thousands of Australian women were lonely. Their husbands or boyfriends were overseas in the armies of the Middle East or in New Guinea, or in Japanese prisoner-of-war camps in Indonesia or Malaya. Or they were dead. Many of the young Americans in Australia had just come from the battle-zones and soon would be returning. They made the best of their rest and recreation leaves in Australia. The Australian girls enjoyed the good times they offered. Old fashioned inhibitions were cast aside.

Antagonism between Australian and American troops in Australian cities was played down by officials for obvious reasons but reached its peak in November 1942. There were street battles in Brisbane. Brawling soldiers used fists, boots, belts and bottles. Shopfront windows smashed. Civilians ran for safety.

The people of Brisbane were startled by the way American

service police began swinging their long batons at every head within reach. Their indiscriminate savagery in law enforcement was reminiscent of Hollywood movies. Their bruised victims, Americans and Australians, were thrown into trucks for removal to lock-up or to hospital.

In north Queensland the soldiers in two troop trains – one full of Americans going south for leave and the other carrying Australian infantrymen back to the embarkation port of Townsville – stopped at signals alongside each other. The story goes that soldiers began exchanging friendly banter about women,

Lieutentant Colonel Blackween and actor John Wayne at Albion Park races in Brisbane, 27 December 1943 (Courtesy John Oxley Library).

and then following insults, swarmed into each other's trains to fight it out.

The troop train fight was mentioned later in File CA947, Security Service, Queensland, marked 'Letters of Interest 26/2/44'. It described an alleged battle in which American soldiers used knives and Australian troops used bayonets. An alleged casualty count had 36 Americans and 19 Australians killed. The Security file claimed this was a fable but said it was extraordinary that so many descriptions of it agreed faithfully in the essential details.

War historian, Dudley McCarthy, recalled many years later that he witnessed a large number of American sailors fighting Melbourne policemen outside Spencer Street Railway Station. McCarthy, an infantry major, and in uniform, was going to the policemen's assistance when police reinforcements arrived. Escalation of small incidents like that quickly occurred when large numbers of servicemen from both countries were on leave in cities or towns.

Street battles between Australian and American servicemen occurred often in the town of Cairns in the far north of Queensland. Some of these undoubtedly were started by Australians who had been drinking. A more serious episode was an Australian commando-style raid on American navy headquarters at Bolands Corner on Spence and Lake Streets. The Australians had planned their attack with military skill and carried it out with professional thoroughness. It was claimed later that the Australian infantrymen were led by their NCOs. The Australians withdrew after inflicting considerable damage to the interior of the building and to American personnel.

L. F. Jeffrey, now resident in the small town of Texas in Queensland was there:

> US military policemen carrying submachine guns rounded up all American personnel in Cairns and got them out of town. Next morning an American sailor was back on duty outside US navy headquarters in Cairns, swathed in bandages and sticking plaster. The town's

school band, which marched through Cairns on Saturday mornings, stopped on Bolands Corner. The band played God Bless America and the bandaged American sentry stood rigidly at attention.

These incidents were not reported in the censored Australian newspapers but spread through the camps by word of mouth, becoming more exaggerated with each retelling. They caused consternation among senior Australian and American officers who had expected electricity between hot-blooded soldiers in full training for war, but not vicious hostility.

The Australian Command investigated the causes of clashes between Australian and American troops on leave and submitted a report to Prime Minister Curtin and General MacArthur. The Australians resented the American's higher rates of pay and smarter uniforms. The report stated that preference given to Americans in the cities by taxi drivers because they had the most money angered Australian troops on leave. Drunkenness also caused some of the brawling. The American habit of caressing girls in public, and their boasting and taunting to aggravate Australian soldiers' attitudes received unfavourable comment.

On the night of 26 November 1942, the inter-army friction climaxed outside the American Post Exchange in Brisbane. It began with an exchange of insults and threats between US military policemen and Australian soldiers. One of the Americans opened fire with a carbine at close range, killing one Australian and wounding eight others.

The following night, between eight o'clock and midnight, the city streets of Brisbane became a hunting ground. Bands of Australian soldiers attacked and beat up every American they could catch. Of those Americans injured, 11 were taken to hospital, including four officers. Another ten were less seriously hurt. (*Official War History* 1942–43, D. McCarthy Appendix 3.)

Australian investigators, reporting on the riots, deplored the American habit of drawing a knife or a gun during quarrels.

Americans seemed to have homicidal tendencies. Australians, when angry, used fists or boots or occasionally a bottle, but in Australia only criminals used guns or knives – until the Americans arrived.

The Australian Army lectured its soldiers going on leave about their nation's present and future relations with the United States, stressing the importance of getting along well with the Americans. General MacArthur rejected a suggestion that he should order similar lectures for his own men. MacArthur also turned down an Australian suggestion that there should be some integration of Australian and American units for better understanding. The General's disinclination to co-operate was received by the Australian Army Command and by Prime Minister Curtin without official comment.

Cordial Relations

In the war-zones, relations between Australian and American servicemen were cordial. Sometimes it was difficult to identify the troops of one nation from those of the other. The Australians had gradually re-equipped themselves with a large amount of American battle-gear.

Two troopships left the United States for the Philippines early in 1942 but never got there. A GI on one of the troopships, A. J. Bradshaw, living in the Melbourne suburb of Heidelberg, 43 years later, recalls what happened. Bradshaw was from Cordallis, Oregon.

> Our ships were diverted to New Zealand and we waited off Auckland for one week. No one was allowed ashore and we had no news of what was going on. We sailed again but still no news about where we were headed.
> One morning all troops were ordered below decks and were told to get into battle gear. They even issued ammunition to us – so we knew we were about to land on hostile territory somewhere. No one told us a damn thing. Not even the officers knew anything.

This utility Truck 'A Model Ford (1927)' appeared to be in imminent danger of collapsing as more than a score of Australians and Americans used it as a platform watching the men of the 7th Division, an elite A.I.F. unit which had seen action in Greece, Crete, the Western Desert and Syria. A quarter of a million people were estimated to have seen them march through Brisbane on 8 August 1944 (Courtesy John Oxley Library).

A fellow from the South told me he would get himself a Jap before I did and I said to him you're on. We were trying to make the best of it, you know.

Well they finally allowed us up into the sunshine again and we are in port and there are people on shore strolling about and whistling and shouting out to the ships as if the war was a million miles away. We were being landed in Melbourne.

That was in March 1942. We must have been the first US troops to reach Australia in a large group. They put us in trains to go to a camp near Seymour.

Word of our arrival must have spread. Thousands of

people came out to see us. They were singing and shouting and lined the railway in some places to see us pass. They were waiting for us on railway stations with sandwiches and cakes and gave us bottles of beer which we didn't think was anything special until we learned beer was rationed.

We went into a camp near Australian troops and got along fine with them. We brought some in to have dinner with us and in return they invited us over to their wet canteen for drinks. We weren't paid in two months and I was broke so I didn't want to sponge by accepting their offer to drink with them. An Aussie soldier found out why I wasn't drinking so he made me take a loan of five pounds until I could pay him back when I had it. He was only a private. Five pounds was a good bit of money.

Through introductions from Australian soldiers at his camp, Bradshaw met an Australian girl named Glynda – 'She's still my loving wife'.

Had he experienced jealousies or quarrels between Australian and American troops?

We heard there was a big battle between Australian troops and a Negro outfit in Melbourne but speaking personally all I ever got from Australians was help and affection and that included the battle areas. We were right beside them in New Guinea.

Fighting in New Guinea with the US 41st Infantry, Bradshaw was wounded twice. He still carries pieces of shrapnel too deeply embedded in his body to be removed.

It was 1947 before Bradshaw was able to return to Australia to his wife, Glynda. There was another delay of one year for transportation home to America.

By the time the year was up we were expecting an

addition to the family and I was teaching school in Melbourne so we decided to give it another 12 months in Australia. We never did leave.

The Bradshaws have four children and five grandchildren. Joe Bradshaw is retired now. He has been back to the United States four times with members of his family.

Did he have any general observations to offer about his life in Australia?

Australia has changed a lot since 1942 and so has America. Perhaps Australia has had too many immigrants in too short a time and that has been responsible mainly for the changes that have taken place.

I didn't care for some changes I saw in the United States. You can buy fun but not happiness. . . I'll tell you what – public toilets in Australia used to be awful. They've got better. . . Funny thing that. . . public conveniences in the United States have deteriorated. Is that significant? You asked for observations and that's one of them.

Joe Bradshaw laughs.
Was Bradshaw a naturalised Australian?

I'm still a US citizen. Certain things happened over the past 40 years and I sometimes thought if they got any worse I wouldn't stay here. Also, it could have got to the point where I was declared an undesirable immigrant.

They don't care about it at the RSL Club in Melbourne where I'm a member. What the heck, I'm now 72 years old.

MacArthur

No American has ever been more warmly welcomed anywhere in the world than was General Douglas MacArthur when he

*Private Joe Bradshaw with his future
wife, Glynda, in front of the Melbourne
Cricket Ground at the beginning of the
football season in May, 1942. It was
their engagement day.*

*When Joe Bradshaw married Glynda
Ferguson in 1946 he was a Lieutentant
– Commander of the US Army Trans-
port Corps.*

arrived in Australia in March 1942 and was appointed Supreme Commander of Allied Forces in the Pacific. He was a fine military figure, tall and patrician, stern and impressive. The Australian public promptly adopted him as a symbol of security at last. He personified the American Eagle, Uncle Sam, the Hope of the Free World, Ultimate Victory.

One of General MacArthur's own staff officers was to describe him afterwards as a brilliant, but temperamental egoist – a handsome man who could be as charming as anyone who ever lived, or completely indifferent to the needs and desires of those about him. Australians only saw and admired his obvious virtues.

When he reached Australia, MacArthur was pale and thin. His drawn features indicated the ordeal he had suffered in the siege of Corregidor. He would not have been human had he not been stunned by the enormity of his defeat in the Philippines. It had been one of the most decisive in American military history. Much was being made of the courage of the defenders of Corregidor and Bataan, but behind all that was the unavoidable truth. The Japanese had conquered. They had killed or were capturing all of MacArthur's forces in the Philippines down to the last soldier.

During his first month in Melbourne, General MacArthur must have been undergoing a trauma of aftershock, a private nightmare of reassessment and readjustment. If that were true, his outward air of calm was an achievement of courage. His manner remained one of resolute composure at all public occasions.

To hold his new base in Australia he had under his command only 25 000 American troops and the deplorably under-equipped Australian Home Army, two-thirds of them raw militiamen. MacArthur had to compete for American supplies and reinforcements against the urgent priorities of Allied generals in Russia and North America.

In asking for help, MacArthur tried to convey to Washington that the Australian troops under his command were unreliable.

General Douglas McArthur and Lieutenant General Eichelberger in Rockhampton, Queensland, 1943 (Courtesy John Oxley Library).

The Australian militiamen had been in uniform only a few weeks. Equally it was true that most of MacArthur's own recruits were not yet soldiers. In August 1940, the United States Army in America had totalled only eight infantry divisions, with one cavalry division and one armoured division. By December 1941, US total forces had risen in number to 1 657 000 men. By April 1942, this number had risen again to 2 500 000 men. The training of the American Army could not keep up with such rapid mobilisation.

During that early period of 1942 when MacArthur was trying to strengthen his army in Australia, President Franklin D. Roosevelt was preoccupied with winning the war in Europe. A biography of Roosevelt, written by James McGregor Burns, recounts that the President became so worried about the slow deliveries of vital war materials to Russia that he told one of his advisers in a sudden outburst of impatience: 'I would rather lose Australia and New Zealand than leave the Russians without American supplies'. It was another example of a hard fact that continued to elude the political leadership of Australia – that America's global interests always came first with the United States. Sometimes those American priorities did not coincide with Australia's best interests.

During his stay in Australia, General MacArthur regained his balance. His ability as a military tactician rekindled and blazed into brilliance. . . He was vain. He was a showman. Often he did not give others the credit they deserved. But MacArthur was the general who arrived in Australia with nothing, yet built and directed a victorious army in an island-hopping campaign that placed the war back on Japan's front doorstep.

Members of the Australian War Cabinet were impressed by MacArthur's readiness to make proclamations of policy on behalf of his country. MacArthur attended most meetings of the War Cabinet and at their conclusion liked to dictate, in the presence of the Australian politicians, his despatches to his Government in Washington. Often these messages were couched in such imperious language that his Australian listeners wondered at his audacity. Frank Forde, an Australian cabinet minister, said later: 'No Australian general would have dared to talk to his own Government like that'.

The Battle of the Coral Sea

Wartime censorship prevented the public from receiving full information about what happened in 1942 and protected Australians from the full fright of their narrow escape. The battles of the Coral Sea and Midway were won in the Pacific, out of sight and sound of the Australian mainland like all those

American sailors leaving for the USA on Watsonia *from Bretts Wharf, Brisbane, 25 October 1945 (Courtesy John Oxley Library).*

other foreign wars. It was difficult for Australians to accept later that the Battle of the Coral Sea had been fought partly from the Australian mainland and had been the beginnings of a last-ditch stand. (Official Australian War Records: A flight of nineteen US bombers based at Townsville on the Australian mainland mistakenly bombed two Australian cruisers from a high altitude during the battle but missed.) Had a Japanese force got through to the Australian coast the civilian population of north Queensland would have had heavy casualties. Had the Japanese taken Port Moresby, the invasion of northern Australia across the Torres Strait would not have been more than a short step.

The Executive Director of the Australian-American Association, Bruce Watson, was interviewed for this book in March 1985. He said that the Australian education system was partly to blame for public disinterest in Coral Sea Week (from May 4 to May 6 each year) to commemorate the saving of Australia from invasion. Watson claimed that new generations of young Australians learned almost nothing at school about the significance of the battles of the Coral Sea and Midway.

The Australian – American Association was formed in 1941. The Association helped organise entertainment for American troops in the Second World War and again in the Vietnam War. The Association launched a subscription drive to build a memorial in Canberra to the United States after the war and people in northern Queensland over-subscribed by double the target amount. The Coral Sea Week commemorations were first organised by the Association – which continues to promote good relations between Australia and the United States.

Looking Back
After the war, 12 000 Australian brides went to the United States to join their American husbands. American servicemen left Australia vowing that they would return to live there permanently.

We met one of them in the airport transit lounge in Honolulu in 1982. He was on the wrong side of 60, bald and overweight.

Radioman First Class R.B. Roach, US Navy, and his bride Miss Reita Cole-Clarke, leaving the Albert Street Methodist Church in Brisbane, 11 December 1943. They have settled in the USA (Courtesy John Oxley Library).

(Surname withheld on request but he said he was Bob. He worked with the city fire department in Chicago until his recent retirement.) His conversation went like this:

After my wife died I was a lonesome widower for a couple

of years. Then I started thinking about Australia again. I had this girl in Brisbane in 1942. I was only 22 years old at that time and I was in the marines. Her name was Maureen. We promised we would write to each other but neither did. After the war I returned to the States and got my discharge from the marines. I became caught up in all the new and exciting things happening. Then I settled down, married and raised a family. You know how it happens? I have no complaints. But I had to see Australia again.

I located Maureen's brother in Brisbane by looking up the telephone directory. He told me what her married name was and where she was living. He told me that Maureen was a grandmother now and a widow. That didn't surprise me too much. Time doesn't stand still – unless we're dead. That happened to some of my buddies in the war. Still in their twenties forever.

Her brother warned Maureen I was coming and I went out to her home in Brisbane. She was still real nice for her age. I would have recognised her. She must have had more trouble finding me again. When she last saw me in 1942 I was as thin as a match and had all my hair.

I love that lady for what she said to me. With her first words she brought us right back together again. Maybe it will sound strange to you, but she said to me 'What kept you so bloody long?' (He laughed). She made me know she had not forgotten how close we were in 1942 and that we still share those memories of 40 years ago. That was wonderful!

Another American war veteran who could not get Australia out of his mind was William A. Kehoe. It took him 21 years to return. Kehoe had been a Petty Officer in PT Squadron 9, and had taken part in Allied landings from Guadalcanal to Okinawa. After the war he became a wealthy business executive in Oxnard, California, but still wanted to live in Australia. He solved his problem by establishing a second business and a second home in Brisbane. His Australian business, Forever Homes Pty Ltd, became as successful as was his business in the United States.

In 1971, Kehoe's Australian business company gained a contract to build Ridgewood, a satellite town near Brisbane, costing $A100 million. Kehoe had to divide his time between his home and business in California and his home and business in Brisbane, Australia. He lost count of his many flights across the Pacific, commuting back and forth. He remained undecided as to which side of the ocean he liked best.

A former member of the US Airforce, Michael Chmieloski, returned to Australia after 40 years to meet families he helped during the Second World War. Chmieloski was stationed at Fenton Field near Darwin with a B-24 bomber group. He listened on shortwave radio to messages from Australian prisoners of war in Japan and Indonesia and wrote them down. Later he typed them in the form of a letter and sent the messages to the families of the Australian prisoners. Chmieloski intercepted more than 1 000 messages and passed them on. 'Sometimes I'd monitor the radio on a Sunday morning and skip going to church parades,' he said.

Chmieloski returned to Australia in February 1984 to meet some of the Australian families he helped when he was a young man. They did not disappoint him. They still remembered.

History repeated itself during the Vietnam War when thousands of American service personnel took rest and recreation leave in Australian cities. Because of public hostility against the Vietnam War – although Australian troops were in Vietnam – US service people on leave in Australia generally wore civilian clothes and were inconspicuous.

Somewhat more noticeable was the visit to Australia by President L. Johnson of the United States during the Vietnam War. He was given a tumultuous ticker-tape reception in Australian cities that overwhelmed concurrent anti-war demonstrations.

5 American Business and Military Bases

American Assistance

Many industries new to Australia had begun during the war, some of them with American help. They had mass-produced machine tools, locomotives, munitions and chemicals. Up to 1944, Australian plants made more than 2 500 aircraft. The influence of American wartime occupation also had left a lasting impact in the use of earth-moving machinery, light aircraft and improved ground transportation. American expertise, energy, and money had changed cities, the countryside and the Australian people. In the Northern Territory, new roads, and airstrips, built by the US forces, had ended communication problems over long distances of the Outback.

Australia had accepted Lend Lease assistance from the United States during the war but had provided supplies to American armed forces to a greater value. She was the only country to use American Lend Lease and come out of it with a credit at the bank. Financing national development and industrialisation now became Australia's major difficulty. A continuation of some form of American assistance, such as Lend Lease, would have been valuable, but the United States was concentrating on the reconstruction of Europe and Japan where cities lay in ruins, and where many millions were homeless, unemployed, and on the verge of starvation. The United States Government did not offer economic assistance to Australia, nor was it requested.

American Investment

Australian governments restricted the importation of finished products by imposing high tariff barriers to protect local manufacturers and to enable secondary industries to expand. American companies, shut out of the Australian market, invested in Australian industries as a way around the tariff barrier. American bankers, ranchers and mining companies also moved to Australia. Government guidelines relating to local borrowings encouraged foreign-controlled groups to seek Australian partners. Taxation penalties also were imposed on foreign-owned companies.

By 1965 two Australian economists, Fitzpatrick and Wheelwright, gave their opinion that too rich a feast of American investment dollars had been placed before their nation. They claimed that it was bad for economic health and growth and for the social and political community of Australia. They were afraid that Australia would lose its 'distinctive character'. (In other ways, too: by 1972, the top five advertising agencies in Australia were American controlled.)

Ed Clark, the American Ambassador in Canberra in the 1960s:

> They forget that English investment money helped to make Texas what it is today. If I buy into an Australian industry it doesn't mean that I'll be able to pick it up and carry it back to the US. It'll have to stay right here.

In private life Clark was a Texan banker.

In July 1967, the American industrialist, Edgar F. Kaiser, visited Australia to inspect his company's $200 million investments. He reminded Australians that although US companies took profits out of the country they also paid big taxes and royalties to the Australian Government. Kaiser told the Australian public: You just can't sit here and do nothing. You are better off by using overseas investment.

A Labor leader, Frank Crean, declared in Parliament that US

investment in Australia was doubling cumulatively every five years. Crean warned that the Australian Government had not been keeping itself sufficiently well informed about the rate of expansion of American investment.

The Mining Boom

Another mining boom started in Australia, bringing Americans across the Pacific. Unlike the gold rush of a century earlier, the Americans this time were major corporations armed with investment capital, technical knowledge and international marketing skills.

By 1971 nearly 70 per cent of all mining operations in Australia had become foreign-controlled, and a great amount of this by Americans.

The Australian public was informed impressively that Australia's mineral production had reached a record value of more than $1,500 million in 1971 and was rising at 25 per cent annually. The Australian public was not being reminded that almost 70 per cent of this production no longer belonged to them. Of course, even a minority share of the quoted figures represented income for the nation in royalties and tax-revenues.

Few Australians stopped to worry how long the exports of minerals would continue to support them in the manner to which they had become accustomed. Exports of farm products also were booming. The future looked wonderful. A lucky country, that was Australia. It did not have to spend much on defence either, as long as it had a powerful friend in America.

Since the gold rush of the mid-nineteenth century, generations of Australians had believed that their country's mineral wealth would always get them out of economic difficulties if all else failed.

On 12 September 1973, J. W. Foots, Chairman of partly American-owned MIM Holdings Limited, the huge Mount Isa-based mining group, complained that the Australian Government was not doing sufficient to encourage mineral exploration. He added:

The mines of 1985 must be discovered in the seventies. Between 1970 and 1985 the world demand for copper is expected to double. This will require the equivalent of more than 39 more Mount Isa mines around the world by 1985.

Things did not quite work out that way.

According to a US Treasury White Paper, American company investment in Australia in mid-1971 was running at something close to $US3.2 billion. This represented America's fourth largest investment overseas. Five hundred subsidiaries of American firms were in Australia and another 1 400 in Australia had licence arrangements with American firms. By 1983 one of America's top banks, The First Boston Corporation, had provided $4 billion in project financing deals for companies operating in Australia, both American and Australian-owned.

Pastoral Interests
The post-war Americans liked buying cheap Australian agricultural land. They began growing cotton, sheep, cattle and rice, and brought new technologies and business methods to Australian food production. They created 'little Americas' in northern and western areas of Australia. There developed districts of American accents, American manners and working methods, American women and kids, American quarter horses, lariats, and American political and commercial attitudes.

In the *Australian* newspaper of 18 September 1971 was the following front page story: 'Americans are negotiating to buy 1 024 000 acres of the Simpson Desert, near the Queensland-Northern Territory border, at a price of 20 cents an acre.' The newspaper explained that the US purchasers were operating through the Overseas Real Estate Trust based in Hong Kong. Cattlemen who had recently taken a look at the Simpson Desert had reported that it was covered with grass and wildflowers after recent rains, and carried good feed for cattle for at least two years.

Australians felt angry about it. When Americans started buying up their deserts – and through companies in Hong Kong – and at 20 cents an acre – it was getting close to the bottom of the barrel. It was too much like the last pieces of Australia being offered in Asian street markets.

In Federal Parliament, Dr D. Everingham, Labor, announced that he wished to offer a higher bid of 25 cents for one acre of the Simpson Desert. Later Dr Everingham urged all Australians to write to the Minister for the Interior with cash offers for government land to prevent it from falling into foreign owner-ship. This mischievous appeal received an astounding response. Every day hundreds of cash donations poured into Canberra to buy one acre blocks of the Simpson Desert. Individual contribu-tions ranged from 25 cents to $10 but there were some written promises for amounts of up to $1,000. Large Australian business companies might not be prepared to risk money outside the capital cities, but the little people of Australia, the wage-earning public, were demonstrating how they felt about it. The Minister for the Interior found difficulty in speaking civilly to Dr Everingham. He was forced to deny strongly in the parlia-ment that the government was putting the Simpson Desert up for sale. He explained that evidently there had been a loose journalistic description of the land for sale through the Overseas Real Estate Trust. Possibly some of the land was close to the Simpson Desert, but it was not part of the government-owned desert. Despite the Minister's denial the public money contin-ued to be posted to Canberra. The government had to employ a special task force of clerks to post it back again. Someone unkindly worked out that it was costing the government 65 cents to return each of the 25 cent bids. The matter did not end there. Dr Everingham and some of his Labor associates announced that in all seriousness they were setting up a people's land-buying organisation. They were going to call it the Australian Heritage Company. It would offer 25 cent shares to thousands of

Americans pioneered cotton growth in the fields of Narrabri and Wee Waa in the north-western pocket of NSW in the 1960s. One of them was Mert Dula, from California, who sits in the cockpit of his Piper Pawnee plane. During World War II, he flew with the Flying Tigers in China and in the 1960s worked as a crop-duster on the Namoi River.

Mert was the first pilot to be given permission by the Australian Department of Civil Aviation to crop-dust by night. He was known as 'Mr Midnight' by the residents of the area.

Australians until eventually the company had sufficient money to buy one million acres of land somewhere on the Australian continent. This land would be saved from foreign ownership and would become in perpetuity an Australian park and nature reserve... The public applauded the idea. It would be an Australian enclave within Australia.

On 21 March 1972, a Labor Member of Parliament, Al Grassby lamented: 'Here's a new figure. Overseas corporations now own 250 million acres while dispossessed Australians are streaming off the land'. Grassby had a flair for drama.

Mineral Resources

An American, Lewis G. Weeks, a highly experienced petro-
leum geologist, was responsible for the discovery of major oil
and gas fields off the southern coast of Victoria. In March 1969,
Australian Iron and Steel Limited, a subsidiary of BHP Proprietary Company Limited hired Weeks to advise them on exploration prospects. Weeks counselled against further exploration in
the Sydney Basin in which the company had been interested. He
recommended that an exploration acreage be taken up off the
Gippsland coast of Victoria. At that time offshore technology
was in its infancy, having been in practice only five to ten years.
Weeks, however, insisted that it would develop to the stage
where economic recovery of oil and natural gas would be
possible over any continental shelf to depths of 50 fathoms.

The Gippsland Basin was extensively surveyed. The results of
the surveys indicated that Weeks had probably been right on
target with the advice he had given. In May 1964 the Australian
company reached an agreement to take as an operating partner,
Esso Exploration and Production Australia Incorporated – a
subsidiary of Standard Oil (New Jersey). A ship-shaped drilling
unit, *Glomar III*, owned by Global Marine Incorporated was
placed on contract for two years for a wildcat drilling program
destined to prove successful. The vessel sailed from Houston,
Texas, in October 1964, and arrived on site in December.

The first well, Barracouta A1, came in on 18 February the
next year. It flowed gas and condensate at rates up to 9.6 million
cubic feet a day. Other gas and oil strikes were made quickly in
the same locality.

American capital and mining skill joined Australian initiative
and British capital in developing one of the greatest iron ore
discoveries in the world in Western Australia. In fact, one of the
largest bodies of ore was named Mount Tom Price in honour of
the late Vice President of the Kaiser Steel Corporation. Price
made the following comment after his first visit to the area.
'There are mountains of iron ore there. It is just staggering. It is
like trying to calculate how much air there is'.

In December 1962 geologists estimated the reserves of iron
ore at Pilbara at not less than 380 million tons of ore containing
60/61 per cent iron. Soon afterwards these reserves were
enlarged to 4 860 million tons of ore of over 50 per cent iron.
An estimate of their money value later was $A38,880 million.

Hamersley Holdings Pty Limited and Hamersley Iron Pty
Limited were formed with 60 per cent of both companies owned
by a British subsidiary, Conzinc Riotinto of Australia Pty
Limited and 40 per cent by Kaiser Steel Corporation of
California. In March 1967, in deference to a public outcry, 10
per cent of the equity was offered to the Australian public in the
form of ten million fifty cent shares in Hamersley Holdings. It
was a little taste of honey to shut them up.

The Australian, Lang Hancock, whose part in forming the
two mining companies was described by one newspaper as 'his
brute force drive and restless energy', was not left behind the
door when cash benefits were paid out from his ore discovery.
He and his partner, Peter Wright settled for 2 1/2 per cent
royalties in Hamersley Iron and Hancock's income rose to
$30,000 a day. But by 1971 he had bigger plans for developing
new ore leases and for building steelworks from which he could
reasonably expect to earn twice that much.

Hancock's philosophy was that of the self-made man. He told
a newspaper reporter, 'I believe, bad and all as it is, that the
greed of capitalism is the only driving force there is'.

In July 1971, the Australian Minister for National Development, Mr Swartz, put Australia's iron ore reserves at 20 000
million tons. As well as being one of the largest deposits in the
world they were among the richest. Millions of tons of the ore
assayed at around 62 percent iron. Deposits of 56 per cent or
slightly less were regarded as low grade. Visiting American
miners accustomed to working much lower grades in the United
States were excited by the value of the Western Australian finds.

Another example of massive American investment in Australian resources was the bauxite industry. Once more, Australians
had to be content with a minority share. The largest alumina

plant in the world was built at Gladstone in Queensland by a consortium of American and other international companies. It was designed to have an output of 600 000 tons annually. Production began in March 1967, and three months later the first shipment of alumina was exported to Intalco in the United States. By May 1967, the capacity of the plant had been increased to 900 000 tons.

Australia was on the crest of its resources boom. A golden age was predicted for all its people. Trade unionists took their share early in higher wages obtained by 'sweetheart deals' with employers, or through strike action. Share-market prices went wild on the stock exchanges as the public tried to get rich by gambling on the prices of mining companies, many of which were speculative and without substance. (The share prices of Poseidon Ltd: 1969, 60 cents; 1970, $214; 1971, $280 – then down to $11. March 1985, $3. Poseidon, though, did have substance.) Behind all the glitter of the resources boom few Australians could discern the truth. Their country was supplying foreign industrial expansion with raw materials but was becoming subordinate to it.

The American Chamber of Commerce in Australia

The American Chamber of Commerce in Australia was created in 1961 to encourage the two-way flow of trade and investment between Australia and the United States, to represent the opinions of the American business community in Australia, and to interpret the point of view of Australian commercial interests to the American business public. More than three-quarters of its members were Australian nationals and 50 per cent of its national board of directors were Australian.

In June 1982, the American Chamber of Commerce in Australia listed ten most frequently heard criticisms of American and other international corporations doing business in Australia. These included:

• The ability of major oil companies to invest in multiple

energy resources and often seen by Australians not to be in the national interest because allegedly it gave foreigners too much control.

• Australians thought that international American corporations could transfer large numbers of job opportunities out of Australia to their subsidiaries in other countries, thereby being in a position to exert undue influence on Australia's national policies, labour relations and the balance of payments. It was also thought sometimes that international corporations made decisions in foreign board rooms that could have major impact on the Australian economy, sometimes adverse.

• American companies in Australia were accused of imposing excessive export franchise restrictions that could impede the export capability of Australia.

• The Australian subsidiaries of US companies were said to exclude Australian citizens from board-room membership or management and to deny equity participation to Australians. Worst of all, it was alleged that large international corporations, including those based in America, could use their power to extract unfair concessions from the Australian Government.

The American Chamber of Commerce in Australia answered all these criticisms. It explained the 'spin off benefits' in employment, technological development, and in the prosperity of supplying firms, that big US companies generated through their operations in Australia.

It argued that multinational American companies were efficient because of their operational flexibility on a global scale and did not willingly close down local operations and put Australians out of work.

The American Chamber said there was a large degree of autonomy in local decision-making in US subsidiary companies operating in Australia. The Australian affiliates enjoyed a great deal of freedom of action in labour relations, production planning, product innovation and development. Only in the area of major capital expenditure were US subsidiaries subject to some degree of control by the parent company.

A survey of major US subsidiaries in Australia had revealed that 22 per cent of their assets were held by Australians and that more than 50 per cent of US subsidiaries in Australia had Australian chief executives. Almost 90 per cent of all senior management positions were filled by Australians. At board level, the majority of directors of US affiliates were Australian nationals.

One of the subjects discussed at 1982 Parliamentary Joint Committee hearings in Canberra was the alleged potential of big American and other international companies to exert power over government. American witnesses said that lobbying was a legitimate part of the decision-making processes of government. Businessmen had as much right as consumers, environmentalists, labour unions, clergy, educational bodies and others to put their story to government.

Witnesses told the Australian Government inquiry of 1982 that the most frequently asked questions heard from potential American investors centred on Australia's trade unions. They wanted to know how business in Australia coped with the demands of 316 registered trade unions. They asked why political strikes were tolerated and why unions sometimes opposed the Australian Government and seemed to get away with it.

The American witnesses claimed that demarcation disputes between Australian trade unions accounted for a disproportionately large number of industrial stoppages. They wanted to know why government in Australia allowed this to happen.

Witnesses for the American Chamber of Commerce in Australia said there appeared to be one law for business and another for the unions in Australia. Industrial disputes affecting sea transport had become so disruptive that they were costing Australia almost $1.5 million a day. This had resulted in the US East Coast to Australia/New Zealand Shipping Conference imposing a levy of 10 per cent 'strike surcharge' on all cargo carried by Conference vessels from the United States to Australia as from February 1982.

A Labor Party representative on the Parliamentary Joint Committee, K. Fry, hit back. He claimed that many workers in the United States were not protected from exploitation by business. Furthermore, Australia did not have a worse record for industrial stoppages due to strikes than had the United States, Great Britain or most other countries. Fry added: 'The last time I was overseas I was stranded in Greece because of a strike by their air hostesses. The whole airline stopped. There is nothing special about Australia in industrial disputes'.

Trade Relations
Australian businessmen and bureaucrats often came away from trade conferences with Americans in despair. Once the Americans took up a trading position there was nothing much that Australian negotiators could do. They lacked leverage in bargaining. The Americans had all the economic muscle all the time, and used it ruthlessly. Australians hoping for favours for the United States' cousin country Down Under were soon disenchanted. Americans did not believe in sentiment in business. They were just as tough trading among themselves.

In the world recession of the 1980s, some American companies and individuals who had bought into Australia 20 years earlier, sold part or all of their holdings. The Australian company, Broken Hill Proprietary, did much more than buy back home property – it purchased 100 per cent ownership of the international operations of the American company, Utah, including copper in Canada, and Utah's deposits of steaming coal and iron ore in Brazil. The deal was good insurance. It had become safer for Australian corporations to spread themselves internationally than to have all their investment at risk at home.

They had followed the American corporate example. But American 'smart money' had begun a retreat from some sectors of investment in Australia.

The early post-war assumption by many Australians that their country would enjoy perpetual prosperity almost effortlessly had been false. Predictions that foreign investment often had been placed to exploit the country instead of developing it seemed to have come true. The value of the Australian dollar had fallen to below 70 cents against the American dollar – more than half its value of ten years earlier and it had also fallen against other currencies. The country had chronically high unemployment and an inflation rate almost double that of some of its trading partners. International markets for Australia's mining and rural output had contracted dramatically, partly due to American competition abroad and partly because of protectionist policies within the United States.

There was a whiff of the 1930s in the air again with the cost of Australia's imports exceeding its export earnings and with the interest on massive overseas debts causing worry. Australia's manufacturing industries had faltered and had begun to decline. They had not lived up to their early post war promise and had never achieved significant export markets like the foreign secondary industries to which Australian raw materials had been fed. The economy had remained perilously lopsided in favour of commodity sales. Because of the unsatisfactory way things had gone, interest rates had risen to record levels, high and often unfair levels of taxation had become a deterrent to investment and to greater worker effort and living standards had fallen for a substantial part of the population.

Americans in Australia interviewed for this book repeatedly criticised the country's low worker output in return for high wages and short working hours. They also commented adversely about a supposed negative attitude among Australians towards the need for self-improvement and ambition to get ahead. . . and they frequently said they had observed a national inferiority complex in Australia.

Well, just maybe they had been contributing towards it. . . if it were true.

On the brighter side, the lower value of the Australian dollar had offered new opportunities for Australia to sell more of its products abroad if it could keep its production costs down. It also had boosted the tourist industry. Tens of thousands of

American tourists had begun taking advantage of cheap holidays 'Down Under'. The low rate of the dollar also had made it possible for Americans and other overseas buyers to snap up cheap Australian real estate and other properties.

An American Opinion
Australian governments boasted almost monthly of national economic growth and the creation of new jobs, but in the context of the complete economic picture this propaganda was unconvincing. Looking for better news we interviewed in 1985, Ronald Gaudreau, 39, and formerly of Newport, Rhode Island, Harvard and New York City. He had settled in Sydney because he had seen potential in the Australian financial sector.

Gaudreau said:

> The deregulation of the Australian banking system recently will increase banking competition here. Banks in the United States like the Chase Manhattan will be operating in Australia. Of course, the financial market here is small for such major international banks but I see that there is a good chance for Australia to become a world banking centre over the next 15 years.
>
> It will depend on a number of things, including what happens to Hong Kong but Australian banking has a lot going for it. Australia has good gold reserves, a favourable time zone for international financial markets and she is also an English-speaking country well understood in major international financial areas.
>
> During the five years to 1985, there have been dramatic changes in the Australian financial community because of the closer involvement of US merchant banks. There are stronger ties with the financial centres of New York, Chicago and San Francisco.
>
> Business in Australia is now more a part of international trading relationships with better access to capital, information and understanding of mergers, acquisitions

and off-shore funding.

But can Australia continue to produce goods that cannot be exported because they are too expensive to be sold overseas?

The other problem is the steadily improving quality of similar goods made by other countries and not nearly so expensive.

Australian industry also has the real handicap of the adversary role of its trade unions in respect of corporations. Unions and employers in this country are not working together to achieve a mutual end benefit. In America I think the opposite happens. There is a considerable degree of co-operative effort in the States.

US Bases and Australian Opinions

Americans in modern Australia include those operating US defence installations. They keep a low profile, as the saying goes, but their presence in Australia over two decades has caused the greatest amount of public controversy since Governor King banned the sealers from Sydney Harbour at the beginning of the nineteenth century.

Many times claims have been made – including some in this book – that the US bases are there for the defence of the US mainland. They would be linked into a future star wars defence system for America and would become a legitimate primary target in a war between the United States and the Soviet Union. According to this body of opinion, US bases are not part of a nuclear defence umbrella for Australia. They are a lightening rod that would attract enemy action against Australia.

On the other side of the defence debate are those who say that the US bases should remain because Australia cannot defend itself and must stand or fall with the American nation. Dr Coral Bell of the Department of International Relations at the Australian National University said in evidence to Joint Parliamentary Committee hearings in Canberra in 1982:

The fortunes of the Western World are enormously
important to us economically, spiritually and culturally.
As an Australian, I feel we should stand or fall with them.
I am not sure that it would be worth surviving in a world
in which they had gone down to defeat. . . I do not think
there is much doubt about it. Australia is a province of
the English-speaking world. I am afraid the capital of the
English-speaking world, whether we like it or not, is at
present Washington.

Questioned three years later, Dr Bell said she would not alter
one word of that statement. 'I think it is even more true now
than it was then'.

Work began on an American communications base at North
West Cape in Australia in 1963. Other American bases were
built later as important links in America's space satellite system
of communications and military surveillance, notably one at
Pine Gap in Central Australia.

The US base at North West Cape consisted of buildings for
instruments and other equipment, an administration block and
accommodation for single men. Above the buildings were 13
communications towers, all of them taller than the Eiffel Tower
of Paris. The base was there to communicate with America's
submarines underwater throughout the Indian Ocean or as far
away as the Mediterranean and the West Pacific. It was on a
desolate part of Australia's west coast, surrounded by low scrub
and the sea. When cyclones raged in from the Indian Ocean,
winds of up to 120 miles an hour strained the base to its
foundations. In summer, temperatures reached 110 degrees
Fahrenheit.

By 1973, a total of 1 100 American men, women and children
were living at the nearby township of Exmouth. Another 400
single US servicemen were residents of the base. About 400
Australians from Exmouth worked there on contracts. Relations
between the Australians and the Americans were harmonious.
Theirs was a rugged life, but congenial social and sporting

activities were available for all. (1985 figures: Three hundred and eighty US Navy personnel were at North West Cape plus family dependants. Australians working there were 48 Navy and 217 civilians. At Pine Gap, 236 Americans, 233 Australians. At Nurrungar, 210 Americans, 193 Australians).

The Australian flag flew at Exmouth alongside the American flag, this being one of the conditions imposed by the Australian Government to quieten criticism that the sovereignty of the country was at risk. Another condition had been an agreement with the United States that the base would be made available to the Australian Navy if ever required.

American Navy personnel came and went without the Australian public knowing anything about it. Starlifters and other long-range US aircraft flew in from half-way around the world without calling at any major Australian cities where they would attract attention. They arrived regularly from Hawaii or Fiji or from the Philippines to touch down at Learmonth, 23 miles south of Exmouth. There was nothing at Learmonth except iron huts, scrub, red dust and usually a few waiting cars and trucks. The landing field was so short that Starlifter transports invariably overshot the end of it before stopping amid clouds of dust not far from the bush.

At the Labor Party's annual conference in Canberra in 1984, some delegates wanted to close the bases now that Labor was in government again. Bill Hayden, who had become Australia's Foreign Minister, addressed the conference and said that the American bases were a deterrent to war. He shouted down objectors and anti-nuclear demonstrators from the general public who had been admitted to the conference room. Red-faced and shaking a fist in the air he cried: 'I have been to the bases, for Christ sake! I know what I'm talking about!' Demonstrators threw punches at him as he was leaving to indicate what they thought of his speech.

A few weeks later, in Geneva, Hayden threatened that the Australian Government would 'review' the American bases if the United States did not become more active in negotiating a nuclear-test-ban treaty and world disarmament. He tried to justify this contradictory statement by saying that Australia could use the American bases as leverage to influence American foreign policies.

Defence Co-operation and Public Opinion Polls

Following the Soviet invasion of Afghanistan at the end of 1979, defence co-operation between Australia and America intensified. There came increased Australian surveillance in the Indian Ocean and the offer of Australian facilities in support of American air and naval operations in the Pacific and Indian Oceans. In addition to an offer of port facilities to the United States Navy in Western Australia, America was given permission to conduct low-level training flights over northern Australia with its B52 bombers. The planes also were given landing rights in Darwin.

A Parliamentary Joint Committee in Canberra in 1982 questioned whether defence arrangements with the United States, and the presence of American bases, had the support of the Australian public. The Joint Committee also examined allegations that Australia had suffered some loss to its sovereign independence as a nation through the presence of US bases on its soil. The results of public opinion polls given to the Joint Parliamentary Committee showed that, despite controversy lasting more than 15 years, Australian citizens wanted the bases to remain. A poll taken in March 1980 showed a 59 per cent return in favour of the United States strengthening its military bases in Australia. A Morgan Gallup Poll, held in July the same year, had public approval of 55.6 per cent for a proposal that the United States should station some of its military aircraft in northern Australia, not merely touch down there.

Other public opinion polls published by the Parliamentary Joint Committee showed that in June 1982, 60 per cent of Australians questioned did not object to nuclear-powered American warships or submarines visiting Australian ports. Only 29.9 per cent were against. Another 10.2 per cent were undecided. A poll by *The Age* newspaper of Melbourne, in October 1982, found a 58 per cent majority of public opinion in agreement with US naval visits to Australian ports, even though carrying nuclear weapons.

Public opinion polls early in 1985 indicated that anti-American Labor radicals were out of step with the majority of Australian voters. Spectrum Research, commissioned by *The Australian* newspaper, found that 66 per cent of intending Labor voters surveyed agreed there was a need for Australia to have a defence alliance with the United States. Of the total number surveyed 73 per cent supported the American alliance.

ALP Policy
In an editorial on 9 February 1985 *The Australian* commented:

> The Federal Government's refusal to honour its under-taking to help the United States to carry out its proposed tests of the MX missile is a clear breach of the spirit of ANZUS... When the Australian people elected the ALP to government they did not imagine that they were voting for pacificism. They chose the ALP in spite of, not because of, its endemic neutralism and anti-Americanism ... Cabinet should have no doubt about the peril to our national interest which would result from any further weakening of our alliance with the US. It should also realise that, if it does anything which could bring about such a result, it will set itself against the great majority of the Australian people.

The Parliamentary Joint Committee issued a report finding that the US bases in Australia were appropriate in the context of Australia's responsibilities under the ANZUS Treaty. The Committee also reported that there was no 'unacceptable' loss of Australian sovereignty arising from the presence of the bases and their facilities. Eight Labor Party members of the Joint Committee dissented in regard to the operations of the American base at North West Cape. They wanted new procedures, and an agreement with America that would guarantee that the American base at North West Cape would not involve Australia in war without the country's consent. That sounded like strong stuff, but nothing else happened.

At the National Conference of the Australian Labor Party in Canberra in July 1984, delegates from Western Australia said they were worried that the United States Navy in the Indian Ocean was using Fremantle as a substitute home port. The conference, maintaining a careful balance between radical and moderate elements of the Labor Party, agreed to a compromise proposal that the number of US ships calling at Fremantle would be 'watched'. It was a meaningless promise without definitions. It seemed to satisfy Labor radicals but obviously did not please US observers in Canberra.

Officials of the Reagan Administration in Washington had told Australian diplomats in 1982 that there was an alarming streak of anti-Americanism in the policies of the Australian Labor Party.

Did Americans in Australia include members of the CIA?

In 1975, Queen Elizabeth's representative in Australia, Governor General Sir John Kerr, had used powers never before exercised to dismiss Prime Minister Whitlam from office. Soon stories began to circulate that America's Central Intelligence Agency had engineered Whitlam's downfall. They persisted. Just before Christmas in 1982, Professor James A. Nathan, of the Political Science Department of the University of Delaware, said it might take a Congressional investigation to get to the truth about allegations that the CIA had sabotaged a Labor Party government in Australia.

Nathan claimed that the Australian controversy dated back to 1972 when Whitlam had withdrawn Australian troops from Vietnam and denounced President Nixon over the bombing of Hanoi. Nathan said that Whitlam had aroused deep hostility within the US intelligence community which viewed the Australian Labor Party and its politics as, at the best, benighted accomplices to Soviet undertakings.

This was rejected by Senator Daniel Patrick Moynihan, Vice-Chairman of the US Senate Intelligence Committee. He said his committee had received information about the allegations and had considered it. Senator Moynihan added that there was no reason, in his committee's opinion, to pursue these charges further.

Future Relations
How should Australia handle its future relations with the United States? What should be its policies? It is worthwhile quoting more of the evidence given at hearings held by the Joint Parliamentary Committee in Canberra in 1982.

Dr Thomas Millar, Australian National University stated:

> It seems likely that by the end of this century there will be at least a billion more mouths to feed in the area from Pakistan to Indonesia and Japan. Indonesia will have a population of almost 200 million, the Philippines of close to 100 million, and China, Bangladesh, India and Pakistan will add up to probably around 3 billion. It seems inevitable that there will be pressures on Australia to share its extensive resources more widely and more cheaply. These pressures will take a political form but they could take other forms as well.
>
> In these circumstances it would be the height of folly for Australian foreign relations not to be strongly oriented to the existing twin policies; maintaining the American alliance relationship and building a network of friendly associations with countries of the Third World.
>
> It is conventional wisdom in some quarters to deplore Australian deference to American wishes and to see us as an echo, a satellite, an agent of American financial, political and strategic power. I deplore the Australian tendency to use the American alliance as a substitute for our own efforts, as a means of getting defence on the

cheap. But a little research shows that it is just not true that Australia consistently defers to American pressures or policies or that Australia is a favoured recipient of American goodwill.

Dr Glen Barclay of the University of Queensland told the Joint Committee:

> Australian governments have traditionally displayed little concern with rationality or credibility in the formulation of defence policy. They had become more concerned with keeping it cheap. It is not an approach calculated to qualify a nation for either alliance or independence.

Dr Desmond Ball of the Strategic and Defence Studies Centre, Australian National University:

> The American defence connection brings undeniable benefits to Australia in terms of intelligence exchange and access to advanced weapons technology, as well as perhaps providing some security guarantees. It is a connection which neither the Australian defence establishment nor the Australian public would be prepared to abandon lightly.
> However, the United States connection also has costs, risks and constraints. The inroads into Australian sovereignty, the likelihood of being a nuclear target, and the obstacles placed in the way of more independent defence and foreign policies are each extremely serious, negative features of the United States connection. They should be continuously monitored by Australia and the costs and benefits should be periodically assessed.

An American witness at the inquiry in Canberra in 1982, Professor H.S. Albinski, of Pennsylvania State University, emphasised the need for Australians to work harder on making their country's problems and attitudes better known in Washington.

> Americans at large know little about and pay scant attention to Australia. . . In some matters Australia is underplayed in the US, and in Australia the US is heavily exposed, at times overplayed. This intrudes upon and tends to distort the style in which aspects of the bilateral relationship are acted out. It imposes a certain burden on Australia to ensure that its interests are not overlooked and that it is dealt with fairly and conscientiously by the United States.
>
> The US has never sought 'client states'. Australia has to compete with the rest of the world for a share of America's attention.

6 Contemporary American Settlers

The Senator

Dr Norm Sanders from California became a senator for Tasmania in July 1985. Earlier he was a member of the Tasmanian State Parliament. He campaigned on a platform of opposition to the activities of American companies in Australia and the presence of US defence bases on Australian soil.

Dr Sanders first saw Tasmania as a Fulbright Scholar in the mid-1960s. He worked there towards his PhD in Coastal Geomorphology and met his Tasmanian-born wife, Jill.

Sanders returned to the United States. At various times he was a commercial pilot in Alaska, a researcher with the National Aeronautics and Space Administration, and an Associate Professor of Geography at the University of California. He was always interested in conservation issues and became embroiled in a controversy with the administrators of the University of Santa Barbara over some of his outspoken comments and militant actions.

He abandoned his academic life in California, set sail in a small boat across the Pacific and returned to Tasmania.

> I felt a sense of loss when I ceased to be a US citizen. You see I was 42 years old when I left the United States. I'd had a complete and successful life there. But having settled in Australia permanently I realised I had an obligation to fully involve myself in my new country

andbecome a legally naturalised Aussie, so I took out citizenship papers in Hobart.

Sanders said it was not always easy being an American in Australia. A love-hate attitude existed towards the United States, and when things were going wrong between the two countries American residents sometimes felt that Australians wanted to take it out on them. The fact that Sanders had become a naturalised Australian citizen on 4 July 1978, did not protect him from this. His American accent remained strongly identifiable.

In 1980, Dr Sanders won a seat in the Tasmanian Lower House of parliament by campaigning against plans by the Hydro-Electric Commission to build a dam over the Franklin River. Eventually the issue exploded into world news.

The Australian Federal Government used its over-riding powers to stop the project.

In April of 1985, Sanders' election to the Australian Senate was front-page news in the Wall Street Journal, a paper read by two million Americans. He was quoted as saying he wanted to make Australia what America was before it lost its way. This statement caused the following reaction: 'About 20 Americans from all over the United States wrote and asked me how could they join me in Australia'.

When Norm Sanders was asked what advice he would give to Americans newly arrived in Australia, he suggested:

They should take time to learn what Australia is really like. Americans first coming here think that it's just like home. That first impression is superficial and misleading. They begin to learn that the first time they step off a sidewalk and look in the wrong direction for oncoming traffic.

Americans have to learn that despite the similarities of language and in the appearance of the people and the cities, Australia is a foreign country. There are many big differences. For example, Australia is a mixture of capitalism and socialism. To me, coming from America, Australia seems a very socialistic state.

I cannot imagine a United States government having a nationalised railway system, shipping line or an airline, the way we have in Australia. That makes the Liberal Party of Australia just as socialistic when it is in government as the Labor Party. Yet the Labor Prime Minister, Bob Hawke, could get away with being even more conservative than the former Liberal Prime Minister, Malcolm Fraser. The Labor Party accepted a lot of

Senator Norm Sanders Outside Parliament House, Canberra, July 1985, following his election to the Senate.

campaign money from the uranium producers in Australia. This was revealed in the papers they filed for their campaign funds.

Elected representatives of the people in the US government are the elected lobbyists for the people who own them, and they represent those people in the government as their highest priority. They are unpredictable unless you find out who owns them. They will fight valiantly on all manner of national issues, according to their intellects and conscience, but toe the line whenever something before the government affects the special interests they represent and by that I mean the special interests of those who own them. Their owners pull in their debts when those special interests crop up.

Now that Sanders was in the Australian Parliament as a member of the Democratic Party and not as a maverick independent, did he think he would have to learn to become politically pragmatic and toe the party line? He replied:

The Democrats in Australia are a late twentieth century group. They are not a 1920s party like the Australian Labor and Liberal parties. Those political organisations try to impose on their members an authoritarian discipline that allows little scope for individualism. That is alien to the way I was taught in the United States.

Did Sanders think that Australian politicians owed electoral debts to the special interests who helped to get them elected?

Not nearly to the same extent. Australian politicians may have commitments to special interests on a political party basis but that's much different from representing business companies or industries or something else in Parliament on the basis of their electoral support to the individual – often surreptitious support, as happens in America.

In the Wall Street Journal, Sanders advocated that Australia should sever its military alliance with the United States and get rid of US defence bases on Australian soil.

> I served in the US air force in the Korean War and later worked on systems for guiding missiles to their targets. I began to realise that the targets we were guiding these missiles to were cities full of people who would all be killed – so I got out of it. The US bases in Australia are bait for a nuclear attack on Australia. They are for the defence of the US mainland, not for Australia. Australia has nothing to gain and much to lose by continuing to accept the US bases.
>
> Australian governments also have bought the most expensive and complicated American defence equipment in the name of their alliance with the United States. Far less costly and less complex purchases would have probably done the job of defending Australia much better and could have helped to develop Australian industries which could have been producing some of this simpler equipment. Take Sweden as an example. They are a much smaller country in population than Australia but have produced a first-class fighter plane.

Sanders was asked what he had against American firms operating in Australia.

> They would have to pay heavily in bribes in America to obtain the same advantages from government that Australian governments give them in this country for nothing. American businessmen find the Australians the most naive of people. All they have to do is to blow a little expensive cigar smoke in their faces and these turkeys

(Australian governments) will give them anything in the name of progress. There was an incident recently of Alcoa having to say to a State government in Australia that it was not being charged enough for the electricity it was using for its production. Can you ever imagine that sort of thing happening in the United States?
Australian attitudes are too negative. This is the result of being put down during the country's colonial history. Australia is and can continue to be as technically advanced as any – if we let it happen.

A Businessman's Viewpoint
We sought out Peter Park of Hawker De Havilland, another American in Australia, to reassure ourselves that Australia was not a backward nation in research and high technology – even if it was politically and economically naive as Senator Sanders said it was.

Park was willing to give the matter some thought. He said:

Magnificent research work is being done by government agencies in Australia but unfortunately government does not have salesmen to find markets for the new developments produced by its researchers.
On the other side of the coin, private industry in Australia employs very few researchers.
A third factor in this situation is that a large number of important companies in Australia are subsidiaries of international corporations. Therefore, they have their research work done with their parent companies abroad. Those are the basics of the problem as I see it.

To America and Back
An Australian who became an American citizen was appointed to represent the McDonnell Douglas aircraft company in

defence sales to the Australian Government. It was not entirely surprising that he thought Australia had been wise to co-ordinate its defence equipment with that of the United States no matter what Senator Sanders said about it.

Andrew Patten, 57, left Adelaide when he was 15 and went to sea. Three years later he settled in the United States and attended Yale University. During the Korean War he was a fighter pilot in the US Air Force. In the Vietnam War Patten flew 200 combat missions in Phantoms and reached the rank of Lieutenant-Colonel. For two years he was on exchange duty with the Australian Air Force, flying Mirages.

How did Colonel Patten represent the US aircraft company, McDonnell Douglas, during sales negotiations with the Australian Government?

> A good defence product sells itself. There is no political involvement. The Australian Government takes a lot of time with a large team of its professionals to assess a product like the F18 fighter plane before it signs a contract to purchase. It buys on the merits of the product.

Colonel Patten was in the US Air Force for 18 years:

> My brother was an officer in the Australian Navy and acquired a British accent while attending British Navy training schools. It was a curious situation when we met in London. I was in my US Air Force uniform and had a strong American accent by that time and my brother was in his Australian uniform with a British accent. Few people could believe we were brothers.

Patten returned to Australia.

> I had a lot of apprehension about coming back. What sort of identity did I have? After a while I found it was possible to be both American and Australian. Lifestyles and

philosophies are not all that different between the two countries.

Most differences that do occur are in the workplace. A US employer gets a whole lot more for an hour's pay in America than Australian employers get here. This has an important effect on industrial production rates when we are comparing the two countries. Relations between bosses and employees also are better in the United states. There is more team work.

In Australia, employer/employee relations are antagonistic. I think that this has European and historic origins. The early pioneers of North America left a different legacy and even New Zealand has nowhere near the same degree of antagonism in employment relations that Australia has.

American Women in Australia
We decided to change the subject and speak to some American women in Australia.

Margaret Heaton, from Los Angeles, told us she believed Australia had a long way to go in according women equal status with men. In the United States, she said, it was illegal for employers to discriminate on the basis of sex, marital status, or on other factors not directly related to a particular job requirement. She claimed that no matter what the law said about it in Australia, chauvinism applied.

> You open up the daily newspaper and there are jobs for men, and jobs for women. You can't do that back home. Here a women requests a job and they ask her what her age is and whether she's married even before they give her an interview.

Maureen Maloy from Portland, Oregon, had lived in Australia for 15 years and had two children attending school. She studied and graduated in economics.

> One reason I did the course was because I'd been passed
> over for a job. A man less qualified than myself got it so I
> thought I'd make it more difficult for them to do that to
> me next time. Many women in Australia are turned down
> for jobs in favour of less qualified men.
> As an observation, I don't think there is enough commu-
> nication between men and women in Australian homes
> and not enough sharing. In the Australian mateship
> atmosphere, men seem to me to be isolated in an
> emotional vacuum. They find that mateship is often a
> shallow friendship and not enough to hold them up in
> time of trouble.
> There is a lot of strength in Australian women. My lasting
> friendships are with women in Australia, one of them
> now in her late seventies. I would find it difficult to return
> to America and leave them.

Asked about any adverse criticisms of Australian women, she
replied:

> After they marry or get into their thirties and forties a lot
> of them seem to play a role of domesticity. They no longer
> present themselves as well as they could.
> I don't think Australian women age well. The sun is hard
> on their skins – but I have also seen women in their
> thirties and forties – and one as young as 25 – who were
> thinking middle-aged and looking middle-aged almost
> voluntarily. They had become frumpy.
> American women are more careful as they become older
> and try harder with attractive hair styles and good
> clothing. The emphasis on sport in Australia means that
> women often exercise a lot and build up muscle. I think
> we need to watch our diet to stay slim and attractive as we
> grow older.

Twenty-six year-old Sarah Rankin from Boston admitted that self-assured career women from the United States sometimes gave Australian men the impression that they were hard and brusque, or even intimidating. She said:

> There are great differences between American and Australian women. American women plan their lives individually. They are brought up to challenge and to succeed and not to rest content with that. There is always the demand to achieve more.
>
> The roles of the sexes in America are merging. Greater economic freedom for women often results in the man in a family not necessarily being the principal breadwinner or in some cases not being an income-earner at all. If the woman can fill the income-earning role better there is nothing wrong with the man staying home and looking after house and children – if the couple agrees that is what they want to do. Economic roles should not be absolute but open to question. I think Australian women are still ten years behind women in America in obtaining independent status.
>
> I get frustrated when I see my Australian women friends playing a subordinate role, often pretending to be less intelligent than they are. To do that is demeaning. . . On the other hand, in the world in general, intelligent women do have problems.

What were Sarah Rankin's impressions of Australian men?

> They have a reputation in America of being the 'love 'em and leave 'em' type. I heard in Boston that they were beer-drinking and rugby-loving – the tough, hearty, bush image. I don't know how that started, but Australian men don't have a reputation for romantic sensitivity – or at least in Boston they haven't.

An Associate Professor of the Folk Lore Institute of Indiana, Dr Sandra Dolby-Stahl, had taken a fellowship at the Australian National Library in Canberra in 1985. She said:

> I have found Australians to be refined and polite and quite expressive verbally. My six-year-old daughter and I have had temporary accommodation at a Government hostel and meet many Australian people staying there. That has been an interesting experience for me and I have particularly noticed the kind way Australian people have related to my young daughter.
> Those have been positive impressions. On the negative side, as an American, I expect efficiency more often than I get it. Being a white middle-class American from the Mid West, I find I identify easily with Australians but they seem to quite often think that we Americans are pushy and greedy when I suspect that they mean enterprising. I don't think Australians in general are as enterprising as Americans in general and this produces inefficiencies'.

The policies of President Reagan so upset Kerry McInnes, 32, from Hawaii, that she decided to take out Australian citizenship. She said: 'Reagan was the final catalyst. I had been living in Australia ten years and felt I should do it anyway'.

She was educated at high school in Washington, DC, and at a University in Vermont, and later became a painter. She said:

> I now feel so artistically wedded to the Australian countryside that I could not bring myself to leave. It's the quality of light that gets to me. There is little moisture in the air and colours are not diffused. It's wonderful. All the Australian painters who have succeeded have recognised and depicted this uniqueness.'

Sometimes she regretted what she described as the isolation and seclusion of Australia from the rest of the world and the lackof 'an international consciousness' among Australian people – 'these intangibles'. But she added, 'It's a comfortable life in Australia. . . Perhaps too comfortable'.

Not always, – in March 1985, a bushfire destroyed her home in Queanbeyan in southern New South Wales. Kerry McInnes and her English husband lost all their possessions.

Her friend, Ruth Norton, 35 came from Syracuse, New York. She was a weaver who used Australian eucalypts in obtaining natural dyes for her products.

What had she missed most during her three years in Australia?

'Cold, snowy Christmas time,' she replied. 'It doesn't seem right going to the beach at Christmas'.

Evelyn Patten from Vermont, whose husband is the former US Air Force officer earlier mentioned, established a successful restaurant and catering business in the industrial suburb of Fyshwick in Canberra. She opened the business in partnership with a New Zealand woman. Within a few months they were supplying hot meals to government offices in the federal capital and to business firms. Evelyn Patten said:

> The quality of food in Australia is outstanding. What particularly impresses me is that Australian women, even those who are busy at work, prefer to buy fresh vegetables for family meals than take the easy way out and get frozen packs or take-aways as happens in the United States.
>
> Australian restaurants maintain a high standard overall. Their menus, cooking and presentation of meals often are quite superb, even for comparatively low tariffs.
>
> People dining out in Australia are more leisurely than the States. They take time to enjoy their dinner and the atmosphere of a good restaurant, as people should when they go out to dine. As an American, I noticed with surprise when I arrived here, that Australian diners usually make a night of it by arriving at a restaurant sometimes as early as seven o'clock and staying until

twelve. In US restaurants of the same standard they would turn-over their number of customers twice in that time period.

On the question of Australian men, Evelyn Patten considers that 'it differs in individuals as everywhere else but in general I think Australian men treat their women well.

Her husband did not entirely agree. 'My wife and I went to a club in northern New South Wales in the mid-1970s and I could not get her past the front door', he said.

> The club was for men. Women visitors were segregated. They had a bleak ante-room for women and it had a linoleum floor. In the main section of the club, where the men were, the floor had a carpet and there was a nice log fire. The club had a slot machine on wheels which was wheeled into the ante-room for the entertainment of the exiled ladies. Every 20 minutes or so you could send the barman out to your wife with a glass of beer.

Did he think that segregation of women at social occasions was widespread nowadays?

> There are some Australian women who still put up with that sort of deal.
> Blue collar workers in Australia still seem to prefer the separation of the sexes at social occasions from what I can see. This does not occur at similar social levels in the United States. Women there are more present and more vocal.

Shelly K. Freeman from Toledo in the United States was a nurse at the Royal Brisbane Hospital. She returned to America, discovered she missed Australia too much, and took a job with a pharmaceutical company in Sydney. She told us:

Australian nurses don't have the high professional status accorded to nurses in America. Too often they are regarded as women doing the menial work in hospitals instead of being given full recognition for the important role they play in health services.

Miss Freeman said she disliked what she described as 'the negative attitude' of some Australians – especially towards finding a job during the current economic recession. It was her belief that almost anyone, apart from the physically and mentally handicapped, could earn a living in Australia.

Shelly Freeman said she was part of the American work ethic. 'I'm dedicated to achieve and not waste time.' Nothing made her angrier than to hear Australians asked 'What do you do for a living?', and to hear a common fatuous reply, 'As little as possible'. In the opinion of Shelly Freeman, most Australians were leisure-minded, not work-oriented.

Perhaps too many people in the United States ruin their lives by being too ambitious and too materialistic. But Australians tend to the opposite extreme, living too much for the joys of each day as it arrives, regardless of their future.

She made it clear that she was not wasting much of her time. She went jogging in the mornings before leaving for work, was active in the Girl Guides movement, and used her nursing skills to help a local handicapped child. And finally we met Billie-Jo McCann from Louisville, Kentucky. She had married an Australian army officer with the occupation forces in Japan in 1950 and was now the mother of five Australians and the grandmother of nine more.

Australia has become far more cosmopolitan since I arrived here after the war. It has the same basic background as the United States and any differences between the two countries are interesting rather than off-putting. But when I first arrived I couldn't talk to people on the telephone and understand what they were saying. Australians used words and phrases differently. It was difficult here for me in the beginning and I was homesick.

Thirty-five years later I know that my life in Australia has been a good two-way street, interesting, full, and rewarding. Maybe it would also have been like that had I married an American and lived in the United States. I'll never know.

Then Billie-Joe asked, 'Did you know that two Australians fought with Davey Crockett at the Battle of the Alamo?'

No, we did not know that... Probably they fought with Crockett, as well as alongside him, in the best Australian/American tradition?

Bettina Gorton

The former Prime Minister of Australia, Sir John Gorton, asked if he could write something for this book about his late wife. The following is what he wrote on 5 August 1985:

Betty Brown was eighteen when she left Bangor in Maine to study in Paris. She came down to Cadaques on the Mediterranean to stay with her Rhodes Scholar brother in a house that a number of us had taken for the Long Vacation. She and I decided to get married. She sent a wire to her mother in the U.S.A. to tell her and the reply was, 'Do nothing until I arrive; am catching the next boat.' So we got married in England before the next boat arrived.

It was the beginning of forty-eight years of happiness, for she was the perfect wife. She came into the deepest Australian countryside and lived and worked in it and when we had no money she did not complain, and when I left her to go to the war she did not complain, and when I came back with my face smashed so that I looked absolutely different, she did not complain.

When I decided to go into politics she campaigned with me all over Victoria. Whatever I wanted, she wanted for me and she wanted nothing for herself always. She kept her American citizenship but she never used to suggest doing what America might have wanted. She and I thought alike and she was, in the truest sense, an Australian.

Her three children, whom she largely brought up herself when I was away, are a credit to her.

Bettina was a terrific help to me in politics and particularly while I was Prime Minster. She was a retiring woman and disliked being in the centre of public attention, yet frequently she addressed meetings for me and played the full and active role Australians would have expected of their Prime Minister. What's more, she did it perfectly.

Most people paid no attention to her being an American. I think she was completely accepted by Australians in her position as the wife of their Prime Minister.

Lady Bettina Gorton, late wife of the former Prime Minister of Australia, Sir John Gorton, (1968-71), who was active in public affairs as Australia's First Lady. She was fluent in the Indonesian language and occasionally accepted invitations to broadcast in Indonesian over Radio Australia.

Demographic Data

Demographic Data of the US-Born

At the time of the Census in 1981, there were 32,620 persons in Australia who were born in the United States of America. The male/female ratio was 54:46.

Almost 70 per cent were concentrated in the 12 urban centres. The largest proportions were centred in Sydney (25 per cent) and Melbourne (16 per cent), representing 0.3 per cent and 0.2 per cent of the total population of each centre.

Just over 61 per cent of persons stated their religion to be Christian. Of those persons aged fifteen years and over, five per cent were still at school and 47 per cent obtained a trade or some other qualification. The largest proportions of qualified males and females had obtained a bachelor degree.

Just under 38 per cent of employed persons were professional, technical and related workers. The largest proportions of both males (36 per cent) and females (42 per cent) were in this category. A further 19 per cent of males were tradesmen, production process workers and labourers while 27 per cent of females were clerical workers.

The largest proportions of those employed were employed in community services (33 per cent) and wholesale/retail trade (15 per cent). The highest numbers of both males and females were in community services. Males are also concentrated in wholesale/retail trade and manufacturing.

Of these persons who in 1981 were Australian Citizens, the largest proportion (38 per cent) had been residing in Australia for 10-21 years.

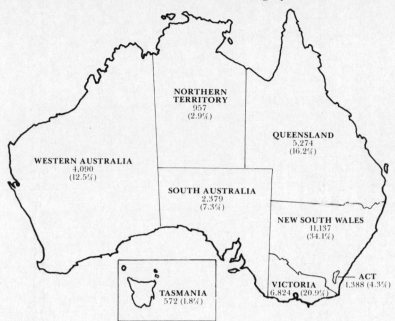

Geographic distribution of persons born in the USA Source: Profile 81, Department of Immigration and Ethnic Affairs 1983.

Main US-born Population Centres Census 1981

Sydney	8 030
Newcastle	222
Wollongong	244
Melbourne	5 298
Geelong	187
Brisbane	2 241
Adelaide	1 577
Perth	2 666
Hobart	239
Darwin	215
Canberra	1 367
Gold Coast	459

Bibliography

Bartlett, Norman, *Australia and America through 200 years*, Ure Smith, Sydney, 1976.

Bartlett, Norman, *The Goldseekers*, Jarrods, London, 1965.

Birrell, James Peter, *Walter Burley*, Queensland University Press, Brisbane, 1965.

Blaustein, Albert and Flanz, Gisbert, *Constitutions of the Countries of the World*, Oceana Publishing, Dobbs Ferry, New York, 1985.

Crisp, L. F., *The Parliamentary Government of the Commonwealth of Australia*, Longmans/Wakefield Press, Adelaide, 1949.

Crowley, Frank *A New History of Australia*, William Heinemann, Melbourne, 1972.

Potts, Daniel E. and A. (eds), *A Yankee Merchant in Goldrush Australia*, Heinemann, Melbourne, 1970.

De Amicis, Jan, 'Australian and New Zealand Journal of Sociology', (lecture) 1976.

Ferguson, Charles *California Goldfields*, Cleveland, 1888.

Hansard, Australian Commonwealth Parliament, Canberra.

Historical Records:

Mitchell Library, Sydney.

La Trobe Library, Melbourne.

National Library, Canberra.

John Oxley Library, Brisbane.

McCarthy, Dudley, *Official War History*, (WWII) Griffin Press, Adelaide, 1959.

NSW Historical Society (various papers).

Raggatt, Sir H. G., *Mountains of Ore*, Lansdowne Press, Melbourne, 1968.

Scott, Ernest (ed.), *Lord Robert Cecil's Goldfields Diary*, Melbourne University Press in association with Oxford University Press, Melbourne, 1935.

Shaw, A. G. L., *The Economic Development of Australia*, Longman, Melbourne, 1944.

Taylor, Griffith, *Australia*, Methuen & Co., London, 1959.

Train, George Francis, *An American Merchant in Europe, Asia and Australia* (letters) Putnam, New York, 1857.

Turnbull, Clive, *Bonanza, The Story of George Francis Train*, Hawthorn Press, Melbourne, 1946.

Twain, Mark, *Following the Equator, a Journey Around the World*, Harper, New York, 1925.

Wigmore, Lionel Gage, *The Long View, A History of Canberra*, F.W. Cheshire, Melbourne, 1963.

Williams Eric, *From Columbus to Castro, The History of the Caribbean 1942–69*, Andre Deutsch Ltd, London, 1970.

Index